NAKED AT WORK

naked
at
work

A Leader's Guide
to Fearless Authenticity

DANESSA KNAUPP

LIONCREST
PUBLISHING

NAKED AT WORK

A Leader's Guide to Fearless Authenticity

ISBN   978-1-5445-0748-4 *Hardcover*
       978-1-5445-0747-7 *Paperback*
       978-1-5445-0746-0 *Ebook*

For my mother,
whose emphasis was, and always has been,
on the spectacular.

Contents

Author's Note

Confidentiality is the cornerstone of leadership coaching.

In coaching, clients confide their most personal, private stories. They trust me as their coach to keep those stories safe as we use them to fuel their growth.

I believe the power of those shared experiences, from leaders across industries and of diverse backgrounds, can drive significant learning for many. Imagining what that knowledge could do for leaders and their organizations inspired this book.

I have told the stories here to the best of my professional recollection to support our collective learning. To share insights while fiercely protecting the confidentiality of my clients who trusted me with their private experiences, I have changed names, industries, genders, and other potentially identifying characteristics throughout this work.

Introduction

"Being naked approaches being revolutionary."

—JOHN UPDIKE, *ON THE VINEYARD*

I thought he'd lost his damn mind. It was awkward, too, because he was, up until this point, one of my most trusted advisors. Mark and I were Georgetown classmates and professional colleagues. We spoke monthly, sharing ideas and resources. As the founder and CEO of my business, I don't have a built-in peer support system. I depended on Mark to help me explore strategy, strengthen my operations, and talk me back from the occasional ledge.

But not anymore. He was clearly out of his mind.

Our conversation had started as our regular monthly check-in call late on a Thursday afternoon. I'd told him

I was thinking about new product offerings, and we'd begun to toss around some ideas.

It was his idea that threw me for a loop.

"I think you should teach a class on confident, authentic leadership," he said. "I don't know anyone who exudes your quiet, grounded confidence, even in the face of overwhelming odds. You are a young, self-made success as a newcomer in a tough industry. You should teach other people how to do that."

The silence hung thick in the air between us.

"I am the last person who should be teaching a class on confident success," I thought.

He kept talking, going deeper and deeper down the rabbit hole of this ridiculous idea. I finally stopped him.

"What are you talking about?" I asked. "I am not confident. About anything. I'm a blind squirrel rummaging around the forest floor; occasionally, I find a nut, but only after a whole lot of rocks. I fail constantly. I'm no golden-girl success story. I started getting smacked in the face by the ball in elementary school, and the hits have just kept coming."

I'm not wrong, and he knows it. I've spattered my personal

and professional history with failure, disappointment, and missteps the way Jackson Pollock spattered his canvases. I've started three businesses and shuttered two. I've built teams numbering in the hundreds that I later had to lay off. I nearly declared bankruptcy. I walked away from a lucrative position as a very senior executive with no backup plan. My first marriage failed.

I've had little to no formal training or preparation for business. I was a psychology major who didn't want to go to grad school. Instead, I pivoted into the cubicles of Corporate America. I never got my MBA; I never even took a business class.

All this should make me cautious, right? Nope. I mortgaged my house to start a food business when I relied on drive-thrus and a microwave for my own sustenance. I took a year off to find myself, which resulted in more questions than answers. I've bet big, often, and watched my chips leave the table.

"I'm no typical success story, and I'm certainly not equipped to teach others about confidence," I scoffed.

That sentence hung in the air.

"What is a typical success story?" he asked. Before I could answer, he continued: "Here's what I see when I look at you: I see a leader who has built three very successful, six-figure careers, each from the ground up. I see someone who can engage with people honestly and authentically without self-monitoring. I see a leader grounded in real experience, who is comfortable with herself and who stands out from the crowd because she is willing to be vulnerable."

He continued: "I see an executive who built such a strong, committed tribe of followers, they left steady paychecks to join her startup. I see a coach whose word-of-mouth recommendations are so strong, clients hire her without ever even speaking to another coach. I see a leader who brings all aspects of her humanity to the table—her professional experience, her motherhood, and her failures too."

"You are exactly what more people need to see. You are exactly the right person to support leaders in today's complex organizations," he finished. And without another word of explanation, he hung up the phone.

That conversation was the beginning of this book.

As I reflected on what Mark said to me, I realized it was familiar content. I've played his role in that conversation far more than once with the clients I serve.

I did it again just days after we spoke, with a talented

executive succession candidate for a major media company. In our first session, we were talking through the frequency and location of our meetings when she interrupted me.

"I have to tell you, I'm not like the other people you coach," she said.

"I don't have an MBA. I work harder than anyone else in the room, but it's not easy for me. It never has been. My father had an eighth-grade education, and my mother worked two jobs. We didn't read much at home. I put myself through school, but I didn't really have a plan. I just wanted to get out of Appalachia."

Her words kept tumbling, faster. "I don't have a great vocabulary. I struggle with my Southern accent. I've been promoted quickly, sure, but I'm not sure anyone here really sees me. If they did, I'm pretty sure they wouldn't trust me with a job this big. I've screwed up before."

"I want you to know, since we'll be working together so closely: I'm different."

I met her eyes and countered, "Here's what I know about you: you were the youngest person ever promoted to your role in the history of this company. You are known for your honesty and your ability to speak truth to power.

Your team trusts you implicitly—they say there's no political swirl with you. You work so hard you skipped a level, going straight from director to VP. I know you're different. I'd argue that your difference is your power. The fires that forged you strengthened and prepared you for this. You are exactly the right leader for this team and these problems."

As an executive coach, I've worked with dozens of C-suite leaders. I've stood in front of auditoriums full of Fortune 100 company senior executive teams and entrepreneurs. I've told them, confidently, what I know to be true: that the unique path each has traveled to this spot, with every disastrous mistake and seemingly insurmountable challenge, has prepared them perfectly for the role they now hold.

And they've thought, no doubt, I was out of my mind.

In the many years I've led and coached leaders, I've learned that every single one of them, at some point in her career, believes she does not have what it takes to be successful. Every one of them has looked in the mirror and thought he isn't enough, that he's fooling everyone. Every one of them has looked back on failures and missteps and wondered, "Who am I to lead this team?"

That internal dialogue can derail many. It can cause

them to work to conceal who they are, to pretend they are someone they're not. The insecurity and shame they feel interferes with their work. Often, that distracted disconnection is something their teams can feel, and it begins to erode trust. The leader doesn't feel present or committed. She misses opportunities to connect with others and does not build strong, united teams. Somewhere along the way, he conceals a mistake or poor decision and begins to invest energy in making sure no one knows. These leaders pay a price for believing the story in their heads: their doubt becomes a self-fulfilling prophecy.

But others, a rare few, come away from the mirror stronger. They engage their inner gremlins in conversation, exploring their stories and background. They look at their histories from a new perspective, reframing them to capture what they've learned. They push through the insecurity to authentically connect with others and build powerful, high-performing teams. Some leaders use the source of their shame and discomfort as the secret sauce that catalyzes transformational change, for themselves and their teams.

Those leaders bring authenticity to their organizations. They pour themselves fully into their role, explore new frontiers fearlessly, and tackle conflict with candor and compassion. Those leaders don't hide their past or fear the future. They are present, committed to the challenge, and ready to support their teams. These leaders become the best of the best.

This isn't happenstance. Leaders have a choice.

Whether the difference you see when you look in the mirror makes you weaker or stronger isn't random; it is entirely up to you. I know this because I have taught it. I have shepherded hundreds of leaders through this process of examining themselves and their histories. I have helped them strip away their armor and show up as their unique, authentic selves at work. And I have watched them and their teams be transformed.

I also know this because I have lived it. That conversation with my colleague inspired me to apply my theory and process to myself. I walked the path I walk with my clients, examining my long-held beliefs about myself and exploring new ways to see my work. And it changed my life.

I am exactly the right person to teach leaders how to lead authentically and with purpose. I do it every day, and I can teach you.

What if you fully trusted that you were capable, resourceful, and whole? What if you knew, without a doubt, you were as qualified and competent as anyone else in the room? What if you stopped talking around issues and instead had real conversations about real problems that revealed real solutions at work? What if your team trusted you with the good, the bad, and the ugly of what was really happening? What if all the noise and swirl of pretense and politics disappeared?

What is possible when your armor and your mask fall away and you are naked at work?

This book will change you and the way you work. It will help you remove what's been holding you back—the old stories, the difficult memories of mistakes and failures, the outdated definitions of yourself. The book will lead you to focus on being the best version of yourself: the authentic leader you've hoped existed but didn't fully believe you could be.

The process in this book will not only power your transformation; it will ripple through your organization. It will support new connection and community in your team and power your results.

At this point, you're likely remembering the story I told you about my background and history a few short pages ago. And you're wondering, "Who is this person to write a book?" That's fair. In this culture of relentless self-promotion, it's a rare leadership manual that recounts all the ways the author has been wrong. And that's exactly the point—I have done this work myself. I want you to know where I started. But for you to trust that I can help you, you should know where I am today.

I'm one of the best executive coaches in the country. I have worked with hundreds of clients in leadership roles across all industries. I have been the trusted confidante to leaders as they navigate the most significant challenges of their careers. In acquisitions, restructuring, and C-suite transitions, I have been, again and again, the trusted advisor in the room where it happens.

I have a deep and experienced background as a senior leader myself, and as an entrepreneur, I've navigated the challenges of startup to sale to shut down. I've pivoted, transformed, and followed my gut into a rich history that serves my clients.

I once thought I didn't have the right stuff to lead. My career ladder once felt much more like a random sequence of trapeze leaps than the powerful web of experience that informs my work and supports my clients. I once was ashamed to admit what I secretly believed: my choices and missteps had caused my career to sputter out long before I reached my potential. I had failed.

I was wrong.

I am a sought-after coach because I know what it's like to fail as well as to succeed. My clients trust that I deeply understand them and thus share information with me that often no one else knows. That trust allows me to support them as they transform themselves. The balance of candor, compassion, and courage born of my own failure is my superpower.

In my experience, all leaders struggle with some level of feeling ill-equipped for the job. It can be a vague sense of something missing or disconnection. It can be the paralyzing thought that you're masquerading as competent and it's only a matter of time before you're caught. It can be anything and everything in between. Those feelings interfere with your effectiveness as a leader.

The trick is how you tell yourself the story of what got you here and what you do next. When you focus on where you are, without investing time and energy in activities that don't serve you, you can deliver results faster and more effectively than you have in the past. When you drop the mask and leave the armor at home, you are better off. When you are simply who you are, open and vulnerable and focused on the task ahead, your team can see you clearly and begin to trust you in a new way. When you lead with authenticity, a new world of possibility and power unlocks.

I can help you move from disconnection and shame to

courage and authenticity. I can help you reshape your past and chart your future.

This book isn't a theoretical exploration of imposter syndrome. It isn't about how to look confident, win friends, or influence investors. It isn't a surface-level checklist of how to lead or include time-saving hacks to help you run your business. There's no fast fix here.

This book is the business case for being naked at work and the proven step-by-step guide to leading authentically. It will show you how to focus your time and energy on moving yourself and your team forward. This book is about how you think and how your thinking influences your actions.

This book is the exact process I've used with executive leaders across all industries to transform their leadership. Doing this work is challenging and takes time. Each chapter builds on the last, combining concepts to help you chart the path of your transformation. I've included the latest leadership research, dozens of real-life leader profiles, and stories from my own experience. I've also included reflection questions and exercises to help you deepen your learning. This is hard work. You're going to get it wrong before you get it right. It's going to feel overwhelming and impossible sometimes. That's okay. You can do hard things.

You can be the engaged leader your organization needs. The work is difficult and lonely at first but gets easier as you practice the skills in this book. You'll learn what the best leaders in the world know: leading authentically is ultimately far more fulfilling than what you've been doing up until now. The payoff, for you, your team, and your organization will be more than worth the effort.

Are you ready to drop the armor and get naked at work? Keep reading.

CHAPTER 1

There's No Perfect Leader

"Perhaps those who are best suited to power are those who have never sought it. Those who...have leadership thrust upon them, and take up the mantle because they must, and find to their own surprise that they wear it well."

—J.K. ROWLING, *HARRY POTTER AND THE DEATHLY HALLOWS*

My mother once called me a spectacular failure.

She uttered the words on a particularly dark professional day. I'd built a business I loved from the ground up and invested everything I had in it. I'd mortgaged the house and spent days and weeks away from my young sons and was now watching it all fall apart.

I was sitting at my kitchen table, sunlight streaming through the window and illuminating the sheaf of financial documents spread out in front of me. I was studying them intently for the fifteenth time. While I was hoping to see something new, I knew the truth. There was no way out. The business owed too much and was making far too little to sustain itself. I had been borrowing to make our payroll and had stopped paying myself months before. We owed our banker, our landlord, and our suppliers, and all were losing patience.

"I'm going to have to declare bankruptcy," I told her.

Facing bankruptcy was a particularly painful moment for me. I'd left a long, successful career in financial services to start this business. I had deep experience with a corporation's view of consumer bankruptcy and, up until now, I felt that only people who planned poorly or made rash decisions or suffered from terrible unforeseen catastrophes ended up in this spot. Bankruptcy wasn't something people like me did. Bankruptcy was a last-ditch effort for the desperate, and yet here I was. The full weight of what declaring bankruptcy would mean for my employees, my business, my professional reputation, and my young family paralyzed me. I sat at that table, tears slipping down my face and spattering my spreadsheets, long after the sun dipped beneath the trees and the day dimmed. It was one of the saddest moments of my life.

I carried that memory with me, as detailed and real as it had been that day, long after I moved on from that heartbreaking spot. It became part of my identity. Long after I returned to banking, rose through another set of corporate ranks, and amassed another rich and accomplished résumé, I could feel the despair of that day sitting heavy, quiet, and omnipresent in the pit of my stomach.

I would walk into glass conference rooms at the tops of skyscrapers and look at the other leaders in the room, assessing them.

Had they spectacularly failed too?

Did they fall years behind in the corporate race because they'd chased a dream that turned out to be a very expensive flight of fancy?

Had they ever lost a bet they'd been so sure of that they'd mortgaged their house and then watched the movers wrap their dishes?

I was sure they hadn't. The other people around the conference table had been to prestigious MBA programs, published white papers on customer behavior, and spent a year in Europe studying our industry from the other side of the ocean. They were smart, accomplished, and successful.

We weren't the same. They were leaders, and leaders were of a certain breed, one that didn't fall flat on its face and stay stuck in the mud. Leaders win. Leaders succeed. I had stumbled, meandered, and ultimately lost. We were cut from vastly different cloths.

I held this hypothesis for some time. Until I didn't.

To be sure, some leaders follow a straight and predictable path.

Rose Marcario, the CEO of Patagonia, graduated top of her class. She got her undergraduate degree in finance, earned an MBA, and spent fifteen years at a private equity firm. She joined Patagonia in 2008 as the COO and CFO, and in less than five years was promoted to CEO. In the time Rose has been with Patagonia, she's tripled the firm's profits. She serves on several boards and has built a culture that functions as a beacon of social responsibility for other companies. Rose Marcario fit my mold of a well-qualified, confident leader.

Sundar Pichai is another prominent leader with what at first glance seems a direct path to the C-suite. Sundar is the CEO of Google and an alumnus of both Stanford and Wharton. He's responsible for the development and distribution of the ubiquitous Google Drive and has been instrumental in shaping how the world thinks about search and document storage.

He also grew up in a two-bedroom apartment in India.

His family of four didn't have a car and, as a child, Sundar often rode the bus for several hours a day. In 1984, when he was twelve, the family installed their first telephone, after a five-year wait. Sundar remembers the day their first refrigerator arrived. When he received a scholarship to study for his master's at Stanford, his family withdrew nearly a year's income from savings to pay for his plane ticket to California. When he first interviewed at Google, he was asked what he thought of Gmail. He'd never seen it.

When I learned this about Sundar, I wondered what he thought about when he first walked into the glass conference rooms at Google. Did he think about how he measured up to the others around the table? Did he compare his childhood self, on the bus or playing soccer in the park in Chennai, to the childhood selves of the other leaders? Did his path feel somehow less than those of his peers? He hadn't had the advantages of private school and a game-day carpool. How did he reconcile his beginning with theirs?

I've since learned he did think about it. He describes his overwhelming early days in California: "I didn't understand the internet. The change was too much for me. I think I was a little lost." As well educated and prepared as he is to lead, as much as he's accomplished, Sundar Pichai, at least once, compared himself to his peers and found himself lacking.

The same is true for Rose Marcario. In 2006, she quit her private equity job after a crisis of conscience. She couldn't reconcile her role in the private equity firm with her values. She traveled to Rishikesh, India, and spent weeks meditating on the banks of the Ganges. She returned to the United States feeling more centered but still very much unemployed.

I've seen this experience, at some level, with nearly every leader I've coached. All have moments when they feel disconnected, disingenuous, and alone. All wonder if they are enough.

We are each privy to our full set of experiences, every misstep and failure and occasional success. That history is never perfect. Each of us at some point believes we aren't the right or best choice for what's ahead.

I worked with a young leader in private equity who struggled with reconciling her difference from her peers. Emily is a bright, engaging woman with a powerful track record of achievement. A graduate of both Harvard University and Harvard Business School, she left Boston to join an elite private equity firm in California. She was promoted early and often and was soon sitting on the forty-fourth floor in a corner office. She is polished, confident, and attractive. She's perfect, at first glance.

During our first meeting, she confessed she was exhausted.

"I'm trying to keep up, but I don't think I can. Everyone else has more time to focus on sourcing and researching deals than I do. My toddler is teething, and he's up most of the night. I can't stay awake when I work late at my laptop. I just keep dozing off, and I know I'm falling behind."

Emily had looked at her peers and realized three things: First, they were all male. Second, none had children or other significant family responsibilities. Third, they each worked all day, every day. She believed that to be successful in this environment, she had to look and sound like the people around her.

Emily worked hard to remove all traces of her son from her work life. When he was born, she was checking email shortly after they left the hospital and was back in the office within six weeks. She rarely talked about him and had a deep list of nannies on call to help her stay late and start early.

"I can't afford to be different," she told me.

We later learned Emily's peers and manager were strongly hoping she'd be exactly that.

Shortly after she returned to work from parental leave, her team had to deliver a pitch in New York. The three-hour meeting required six team members to fly cross-country and return in one twenty-four-hour period. Emily, nursing an infant, couldn't figure out how to make that work and, after agonizing about her decision, asked if the team would consider a virtual option for the meeting. Could they pitch via video?

The team agreed, and the pitch went well. It was a long shot, though, and the client ultimately selected a firm with deeper experience in their niche. The team's physical presence wouldn't have made a difference. When they heard the news, the team members were grateful not to have spent a dozen hours in the air that day.

Two years later, eight of the nine team members remember that pitch as successful because, while it didn't result in new business, it allowed the team to practice their skills at pitching virtually. During our work together, several of

Emily's teammates told me they were grateful she'd spoken up and hoped she'd do it again to save them from some of the brutal travel common to the private equity industry.

But Emily never has.

She is the lone team member who views that pitch, and that full episode, as unsuccessful. She tells herself that her proposal, and the team's accommodation of her request, cost everyone a long-shot win.

Emily is telling herself a story about her difference. Some parts are true. She did ask the team to accommodate her need to be home with her baby. The team did lose the pitch. Those are facts.

But some parts of the story are her interpretation of the events. Her interpretation, or assessment, is different than the assessment of her team members. She believes that the pitch was lost because the team didn't travel. She believes that the team prefers to travel, that the team puts that long-ago loss in her column, and that she now must make up that loss.

At the start of a coaching engagement, I interview my client's colleagues to better understand my client's strengths and gaps. I learned of this wide gap in perspectives when I interviewed Emily's coworkers.

All of Emily's coworkers called her a hard worker and a top team producer. Each also saw she was tired and attributed that to her strong competitive drive. "Emily is relentless." "Emily cares about nothing except work." "When I think about promoting Emily, I worry her pace isn't sustainable." And most interestingly, from a senior partner: "I wish Emily would rock the boat more often. We're looking for innovators and visionaries. She's a great worker, but she does things the way they've always been done. Except for that time when she recommended we not travel to a long-shot pitch."

Emily's negative assessment of that long-shot virtual pitch was preventing her from doing the very thing the senior partner wanted.

Emily viewed this event and its outcome as a set of facts, but they are not.

Facts are provable and immutable. *That desk is three feet wide* is a fact. I can measure it with a tape measure and so can you. *My dog is four years old* is a fact. *I did not travel for the pitch* is a fact.

Assessments are subjective interpretations of the facts. *My desk is wider than most. My dog is full-grown. That pitch was important. My argument not to travel for it cost my company money, and the team blames me.*

If we carefully consider what we believe to be true about ourselves, our history, or our work, we find that most of that information is our own set of assessments. Very little of what we believe to be true is objectively provable.

Paul is the CEO of one of the nation's largest incident response companies. He built the company from the ground up, spending long days at his desk growing his organization and long nights at sites of dangerous chemical spills.

Paul is fifty-four years old, tall and fit, with bright blue eyes and a clean shave. Dressed sharply, in tailored suits and expensive shoes, Paul radiates energy. He picks up his cell phone each and every time it rings, speaks quickly and definitively, and acts fast. He is a power player, and his team and competitors feel it.

Over the years, Paul's company has attracted the attention of several investor groups, which made offers to buy all or part of his business. The money would have been meaningful: enough for Paul to grow the company internationally, invest in ultramodern equipment, or retire to a small island and finally ignore his phone.

He's never entertained an offer.

"How could I?" he asks, sitting behind his polished desk.

"Without a college education, I'd never work again. I can't lose this business."

Paul assesses that his experience growing and leading his company is worth less than a college education. He believes that he can't compete with other, more formally educated professionals in the workplace. And notice that Paul isn't talking about competing as a CEO. He's talking about competing on any level. His story is that without this specific role as CEO of the national company he built, he'd be unable to work *at all*. Because Paul views himself as less than those who are college-educated, he cannot see the enormous opportunity in front of him as anything but a threat.

Paul's path to leadership is less conventional than most large-company CEOs, but there are many leaders with unconventional paths. The truth is, though, as outsiders we don't care much about the paths leaders take to success. We revere the success itself instead of looking too closely at how they got there.

The path to leadership matters, though, because it can shape the leader's internal personal story. Our personal stories influence how we think about our abilities, achievements, and possibilities.

Google's former CEO, Eric Schmidt, memorialized his

coach in his 2019 book *Trillion Dollar Coach: The Leadership Playbook of Silicon Valley's Bill Campbell*. Campbell, a trusted advisor to some of the most famous leaders in tech, started his career as a football coach. He never entered a company conference room until his mid-forties. His first business, Go, was an abject failure: "Go," he would say, "didn't go." Fast-forward thirty years and Campbell's client list reads like a who's who of Silicon Valley game-changers. Eric Schmidt, Sheryl Sandberg, and Steve Jobs all counted Bill Campbell as a trusted advisor and coach.

Bill didn't spend much time wondering if or how his experience as a football coach related to his work in the boardroom. He didn't look at the massive failure of his first venture and think, "I'm not cut out for this." Rather, Bill harnessed the power of his unconventional path. He used stories from the field on walks with Steve Jobs. He mined the Go failure for lessons when counseling Ben Horowitz on how to save his floundering tech startup in the middle of the dot-com bust. Bill brought every step of his path to his work to benefit his clients. Unlike Emily and Paul, Bill didn't allow his background to spin a negative story that limited him. Instead, he embraced it, and it made him stronger.

While the value I've created for clients doesn't yet measure in the trillions, I came to coaching and leadership via an unconventional path, just like Bill. Like Bill and the rest of us, I carry the memories of each step of that path with me.

The day I heard my mother call me a spectacular failure is one that stands out. She was sitting at the table with me, hoping to provide some measure of comfort in her presence. She watched me shuffle the papers, searching for a silver bullet to save me from what was so painfully obvious.

She, of course, knew my whole story up to that point. She watched me pivot from an undergraduate degree in psychology and sociology to a role where I was surrounded by peers with MBAs from prestigious universities. She watched me move past those colleagues and others with deeper work experience or more conventional paths to leadership. She saw me walk away from my golden handcuffs to start a business I was passionate about. And now she was watching it fall apart.

She patted my hand.

"It will be okay, honey. You shoot for things other people only dream about. It's what drives and defines you. You do spectacular things. This happens to be a spectacular failure. You will survive this and go on to the next spectacular win."

My assessment of our conversation and that time in my

professional career has shifted over the years. She never called me a failure. That's what I first heard, but it's not what she said.

Now I can see that, in that moment, my mother was offering me a different way to see my experience. She could see that this failure, as miserable and spectacular as it was, was only one part of my ongoing story. In fact, she said exactly that.

If I had heard her accurately, I might have pulled myself together and used that failure as a springboard for learning and growth. I wish I could say that I immediately became a stronger leader. But that's not what happened. I wasn't ready. I was stuck on the failure. Losing my business made me overly cautious. I spent the months and years that followed second-guessing my instincts and avoiding any potential risk. I allowed that moment to shape my story in a way that limited me. And then, with new understanding and resolve, I picked up the rest of the story and rewrote my narrative. Today, that courage-building experience makes me fearless.

Anyone can learn to lead well. Leadership is a skill to be learned and practiced. Great leaders are not made from one single mold. Many have histories with humble beginnings, big mistakes, and long lists of things they would do differently. Your path to leadership matters most to you. It matters because it is either limiting you or serving you. And you have more control over that than you think. I work with clients on reframing their story to harness the power in it. I show them how to see their stories in the context of their journey and use that experience to serve themselves and their team. I'll show you how to do the same.

KEY TAKEAWAYS:

- There is no perfect leader.
- Many leaders believe they are less than their peers, and that belief is an obstacle.
- We are influenced by facts and assessments but often confuse the two. Facts can be proven and are immutable. Assessments are stories we tell ourselves that cannot be proven and might be viewed differently by others.
- You can reframe the story you tell yourself.
- Your path can be mined for experiences and perspectives that can uniquely contribute to your success and the success of your team.

REFLECTION:

- What parts of your leadership path, positive or negative, stand out to you?
- What assessments do you hold about yourself?

CHAPTER 2

The Game-Changing Equation Leaders Need to Know

"Any distraction tends to get in the way of being an effective gangster."

—TERENCE WINTER

"Bounce...hit."

"Bounce...hit."

"Bounce...hit."

Molly is at a tennis lesson, and her instructor has asked her to watch the ball. It's her first lesson, and she's been so nervous about it she called yesterday to cancel. The instructor talked her out of it and now she's here, learning tennis for the first time. On national television.

Molly is a middle-aged, overweight housewife. She's never been particularly active, and she's arrived at today's lesson in a floor-length burgundy plaid housedress. Her frizzy blond hair hangs loose around her shoulders. She's never picked up a racket.

Her instructor is Tim Gallwey, a tennis instructor on sabbatical from his career in higher education. He's claimed he can teach anyone to play competitive tennis in less than an hour, a claim that predictably has attracted attention and is about to unfold on a very public stage. Television cameras dot the stands.

Tim begins by placing a tennis ball machine at one end of the court. He goes to the opposite end and begins gently hitting the pitched balls back over the net. He asks Molly to watch him and call out when the ball hits the ground and when the ball hits his racket.

Molly is standing to the side of the court, holding a racket and watching Tim return the ball.

She begins tentatively, "Bounce...hit."

After a few minutes, Tim asks Molly to come to center court and continue watching the ball.

"If you feel like hitting the ball, go ahead," he tells her.

It's not very long before Molly steps into the ball's trajectory, swings the racket, and returns the ball over the net. Her teacher says nothing; no praise, no correction. Seven and a half minutes later, Molly is confidently and consistently returning the ball. Tim shifts her positioning, and viewers see he is now teaching her backhand.

In seventeen minutes, Molly is playing tennis and playing it well. Tim has taken over the role of the pitching machine. She's scored her first point against him, and he's covering significant ground to prevent her from scoring again. The grainy footage captured by the cameras that day shows her laughing and smiling as she returns his serve. She's enjoying herself.

That was in the early 1970s, and Tim Gallwey published the experiment and his method in his seminal work, *The Inner Game of Tennis*. Within ten years, Tim had published several more books and successfully applied his method to the world of business. Today, Tim is a sought-after keynote speaker and executive coach. His work aims to maximize the performance of individuals and teams, whether on the tennis court or in the boardroom.

Gallwey defined the framework for the inner game method, but its principles are familiar to us. He suggests that it is our inner process—our self-talk, fears, doubts, lapses in focus, or limiting beliefs—that gets in the way of achieving our goals. His method, outlined in his first and later books, moves attention away from the negative swirl inside our heads and to the task at hand.

When Tim asked Molly to watch the ball and repeat the bounce-hit rhythm, he directed her attention outside her head and into the game. He concentrated her efforts and removed any limiting constraints. Tim didn't tell Molly he'd have her playing tennis in less than an hour; he didn't correct how she held the racket after a wild hit or call "atta girl" after a strong one. Molly wasn't worried about what had happened before she arrived or during the last hit. She wasn't worried about what came next. Gallwey focused her attention on one single thing and let her unconscious take care of the rest.

Gallwey synthesized his inner game theory into a simple equation for performance.

Performance = Potential – Interference

Your performance at any given task—playing tennis, developing strategy, or mobilizing a team—is simply a matter of your potential to perform that task (what you know) minus what's in your way (your interference).

Think of a train on a track. If the train can reach a maximum speed of seventy-five miles per hour, it will achieve that speed unless something is in the way. That something, whether it is internal engine trouble, a train ahead, or a tree across the tracks, interferes with the train's ability to reach its top speed and slows the train down.

In my years of experience as an executive coach, I have not found a framework that better captures how to optimize outcomes for individuals, teams, or organizations. My clients have broad responsibilities, ambitious agendas, and many obstacles. While the train is a simple, straightforward example, the senior leaders I work with face complex, detailed problems. The performance and potential framework reduces those problems to their most basic elements, and solutions often surface quickly.

Jim is the CEO of a large not-for-profit hospital system. He recently sat across from me, struggling with a difficult decision driven by budget cuts and made stickier by the personalities of the leaders involved. During our session, he told me four separate times that the problem he was facing was "very complicated."

On the surface, I agreed with him. His issue involved

members of his board of directors, complex budget negotiations, and a history of tangled supplier-business relationships. Jim had fallen down a rabbit hole into a confusing wonderland of competing priorities, constrained resources, and nuanced human interactions. He was swirling, stuck, and unable to move forward.

As we worked through the potential of the situation and listed the sources of interference, Jim was better able to name what was possible and specifically what was in his way. We used our session to find and rank the sources of interference, and by the end of our conversation, Jim had a list of action items to address each source of interference.

Potential wasn't an issue in Jim's situation. That is the case in the most difficult performance problems my clients face.

Potential is rarely the limiting factor in the performance equation, because issues around potential are more visible. It is usually easy to see what the leader or team doesn't know and addressing those knowledge gaps is straightforward work. Leaders are often accustomed to solving problems by broadening potential. Adding capital, bodies, or bringing in experts are all ways leaders solve potential problems. Reading this book, taking a class, or registering your team for training all expand potential. Expanding potential by learning is often seen and rewarded as positive progress. In many companies I support, continuous learning is a key competency required of leaders and imbedded in the culture.

Interference is what's in the way of achieving top performance. Interference is more difficult to spot and address because it comes in a variety of shapes and sizes.

Dr. Martin Levy understands interference well. Dr. Levy is a professor of orthopedic surgery at the Montefiore Medical Center in New York City. He specifically designed his surgeon training program to eliminate interference.

Traditionally, when a surgeon is training, instructors watch her perform a procedure and give her feedback. The observing instructor recommends adjustments, offers constructive criticism, and praises what the surgeon did well. Dr. Levy realized that conversation of any kind decreased the surgeon's ability to perform. Both praise and criticism drew students' attention away from the procedure to what their teacher thought of them.

Dr. Levy shifted the approach and began to reinforce correct movements in surgery with a dog training clicker, the same plastic handheld device that trainers use to get Rover to roll over.

Each time a surgical resident did something right—picked up the right instrument, or made a neat incision, for example—the observer would press the clicker. A click generated the correct behavior the next time. No click prompted a different approach during the next attempt. Residents quickly understood what behaviors to repeat and what behaviors didn't meet the mark. Over time, the surgeons that experienced clicker reinforcement repeated correct behaviors faster and more often than surgeons receiving verbal praise.

The praise or correction from instructors was interference for these deeply motivated, intelligent doctors. They had enormous potential, but their performance was negatively affected by discussion of any kind with their instructors. The use of the dog clicker supplied necessary feedback without creating a significant distraction.

Dr. Levy isn't alone in his use of a clicker to cut interference and focus the attention of humans learning new skills. Dog clickers have been used to train dancers, fishermen, and golfers. In each case, the simple click gives clear, direct feedback without the emotional baggage that causes interference.

Interference can be internal or external, real or imagined. For a train, external interference looks like a fallen tree ahead on the track. For a skilled surgeon, internal interference is the emotional response to a professor's public correction. Interference can affect individuals and teams. Naming it and addressing it can be easy and straightforward or much more complicated, requiring many steps and significant time.

When I work with clients facing interference, we use Gallwey's performance equation to answer three questions:

· What is the potential for performance?
· What specifically is interfering?
· How might you address that interference?

Once they understand this framework, leaders can often run through this process independently before a large meeting or in a tricky negotiation. Sometimes, the answers aren't obvious, and we address these questions in a coaching session. Sometimes, leaders don't know how to identify the interference they're facing.

That was the case with Harrison. Harrison hired me for no reason. At least, that's how it felt to him initially. In our first conversation, he told me that he wasn't sure what goals he wanted to work toward; he just knew he was feeling off his game. A former Army Ranger, he'd built his consulting firm from the ground up and seen profits double several times over in the years he'd been working. He was a charismatic, engaged leader and well loved by his team.

Harrison had recently hired a COO and was looking forward to the woman he'd chosen taking some of the day-to-day operations off his plate. Three months into the relationship, though, things were starting to unravel.

Samantha, the COO, was whip-smart, trustworthy, and well versed in his business. She jumped in at once, taking responsibility for employee satisfaction and HR issues. She'd set up a new organizational structure and stepped seamlessly into the number two spot in the eyes of clients and colleagues. And then her progress stopped.

Harrison wasn't sure what happened. The COO seemed to like the role, and the team loved her. She appeared engaged and eager to learn. But he wasn't getting the leverage he'd hoped from her, and he had begun to feel that he'd invested significant time and money in her without return.

When I spoke with her, she told me a different story.

"Harrison hired me and told me he wanted me to run this company in the next eighteen months. I was excited about that opportunity. But I'm afraid he won't let that happen. He's deep in the weeds of this business and won't let me in," she said.

"He arrives much earlier than the rest of the team and

spends his morning reaching out to clients. When someone escalates a problem in our team meeting and we plan to address it, Harrison circumvents the plan and handles it himself. When I share my ideas about how to grow our business, he responds by explaining why we've always done it the way we do, and we never try what I propose."

She was frustrated and beginning to think she'd be looking for another role in eighteen months rather than running the organization.

The COO's interference was clear. Harrison was blocking her from achieving peak performance. She needed a plan to give him that clear feedback and step into her authority.

But the COO wasn't my client. Harrison was, and he faced his own interference.

He said he wanted to step away from the business, but he wasn't moving. Harrison and I spent several conversations working to understand why he wasn't allowing the COO to lead. We explored issues of trust, will, and skill. He was confident that she was the right choice and had the ability to lead.

Our conversations revealed that while Harrison wanted very much to step away from day-to-day operations, he wasn't sure what he'd do once he had that distance. If he wasn't in the office by seven, where would he be? If he wasn't speaking at the industry conference, what would he be doing? He had worked more than sixty hours a week his whole life. His identity was inextricably tied to his work.

Harrison didn't know who he was if he wasn't working, and he was afraid to find out. Fear was his interference.

Once we understood the real issue, Harrison and I began to address that fear. We explored ideas for his next chapter. We looked at ways he could broaden his definition of himself, looking into his roles as husband, father, and son. Harrison explored what he wanted next and began to consider opportunities. When we ended our coaching engagement, Harrison had one foot out of the office door, and the COO was feeling much better about her career trajectory.

I ran into Harrison two and a half years after we finished our coaching, at an elite CEO retreat in the mountains of North Carolina. He was a different man. Energetic and engaged, he had recaptured the spark he'd been missing three years earlier.

Harrison told me his COO was leading the full operation now, allowing him time and space to think. He had invested in two new businesses and was excited about those prospects. He was spending more time with his wife and family and looked happy and relaxed.

"Once I let go of the security of running the daily operations and allowed Samantha to lead, I was free," he told me. "It was new and different for a bit, but I found my footing. I've never been happier."

Harrison's fear of losing his value and identity was the interference he faced. Once he named and addressed it, he was able to perform at a different level and so was his talented COO.

Performance = Potential − Interference

The simple elegance of Gallwey's equation stands the test of time and industry. It applies to middle-aged women on the tennis court for the first time and individuals and teams in the workplace. It can address external business and operations problems and more complex internal issues.

Leaders, teams, and organizations can power their performance by adopting the bounce, hit, repeat rhythm of Gallwey's student on the court. Eliminating interference, whether it be a tree across the tracks or an internal dialogue about not knowing anything about tennis, allows performers to reach their full potential.

That might sound complicated, but interference can be anything. Leaders often aren't sure what their interference is and may attribute issues incorrectly. In my experience, though, for many leaders the most common source of interference is shame. We'll address that topic in the next chapter.

KEY TAKEAWAYS:

- The key to optimal performance is maximizing potential and eliminating interference.
- Organizations are typically open to and adept at maximizing potential by securing resources, setting up formal training and mentorship programs, and supporting external learning.
- Interference is much more difficult to address.
- Interference can be internal or external, real or imagined. Interference can affect individuals and teams. Naming it and addressing it can be easy or complicated.
- You might not know what's in your way, but it is worth your time and energy to find out.

REFLECTION:

- What is your full potential for performance?
- What specifically is interfering with you now?
- How might you address that interference?

CHAPTER 3

What's in the Way
Is Probably Shame

"Shame is the lie that someone told you about yourself."

—ANAIS NIN

Dr. Brené Brown doesn't like to chat on airplanes.

Years ago, the well-known shame and vulnerability researcher found an effective way to stop seatmate chatter. Dr. Brown shuts conversations down by telling people what she does for a living. The minute she tells people that she has spent the better part of twenty years studying shame, they suddenly become very interested in the safety briefing or the in-flight magazine. People don't like to talk about shame. As Dr. Brown discovered, we will work to avoid even having a theoretical conversation about that difficult emotion.

Dr. Brown is an author and research professor at the University of Houston's Graduate College of Social Work. Her broad, careful research led her to develop what is now the most commonly used definition of shame: "the intensely painful feeling or experience of believing that we are flawed and therefore unworthy of love and belonging—something we've experienced, done, or failed to do makes us unworthy of connection." In my work with clients striving to lead authentically, we focus on the feeling of being unworthy of belonging, like you don't really deserve to be where you are.

I encounter shame regularly with my clients, but it doesn't always show up as shame at first. Clients certainly don't claim shame. In fact, I have learned that if I label what I'm seeing as shame outright, my clients will categorically deny the feeling. Shame feels too personal and intimate to talk about with a coach. In order to help a client see and own their shame, we often have to have a deeper conversation about who they are and the stories they are telling themselves.

That's how the work began with Sara, a recently promoted C-suite leader. Sara struggled with stepping into her full authority in her new role. She was hesitant to speak up in the boardroom and reluctant to take and hold a position on management-team decisions.

When we first began working together, she wasn't sure

what was in her way. She had a strong analytical background and often found herself ahead of other leaders in processing new information. But when it came to asserting her authority or standing her ground when challenged, she faltered. Even when she was confident she knew the right answer, she yielded to others. During decision-making discussions, she fell into line and backed the CEO and board chair, even when she privately disagreed with them.

Sara knew this was a problem. She wanted to make bigger decisions and take part in strategy discussions but couldn't figure out what was in her way. She'd make a plan to speak up in the next meeting, only to find herself sitting silent once again. Sara couldn't name her interference, and that made it hard for us to address and remove it.

More than six weeks into our engagement, Sara casually commented that she hadn't emailed her mother from her work account since her promotion. When I asked why, she confessed she didn't want her mother to see her new chief operating officer title in her email signature.

"I come from a small town. People work hard for what they have there, and the work is very physical. School isn't important where I come from. Growing up, no one cared that I got good grades. My mother thought if I spent time studying in my room, I was lazy. If I talked about my test scores, I was full of myself. I learned to keep my achievements to myself."

I tugged that thread with Sara, asking, "What does the COO title mean to you?" After running through the obvious answers—more responsibility, a raise, a seat at the table—Sara fell silent.

"Honestly, it feels like I've gotten too big for my britches," she confessed.

Over the next hour, Sara and I worked through what it meant for her to be a senior leader at a large professional services firm. We looked closely at how she reconciled her current role with how she grew up.

What we found was shame. Sara was proud of her new role but didn't want to draw attention to it. The idea that she was flaunting her new role by mentioning it made her feel ashamed and as though she was somehow sitting in judgment of her parents, family, and upbringing.

The old stories about being full of herself and about white-collar professions not being real and honorable work still rang true for her. Those beliefs got in the way of achieving what she'd been promoted to do. If she was a terrific corporate COO, was she leaving her family behind? Could she be both the little girl from a small industrial town in the mountains and a strong leader in a large professional services company? Was she enough of each to belong in each place?

Over time, Sara and I worked to reframe her stories, honoring both how she was raised and the leader she had become. She understood that sharing her achievements wasn't a rejection of what her family believed. Once she did, she was able to step fully into her C-suite role and soon began delivering the value her team expected.

I had a similar experience when I returned to corporate work after the failure of my business. A former leader and dear friend recruited me heavily to take a high-stakes, high-profile role on his team. I accepted his offer only to find myself sitting in his office two months later.

"Where are your guts?" he asked. "When we last worked together, I could depend on you to have the hard conversations. I trusted you to find a way through all the bureaucracy to revenue. I need you to deliver that in this job, and it's not happening. What's going on?"

He was right. I was meeker in this new role, meeker than I had ever been. I was following rules, dotting i's, crossing t's, and trying to please everyone. The problem was, I didn't know why I was different, only that I was. I promised him I'd figure it out and deliver the gumption he'd hired.

I went home and thought about what was in my way. I thought about my interference all the next day, from my early morning shower to my evening commute. Turning and turning on the topic, I finally got to the answer. I was afraid, embarrassed, and ashamed.

I'd failed big in my business. The story I was telling myself was that if I wasn't careful, I'd fail again. I didn't believe I was good enough to lead this work, having made that kind of mess before. I worried I'd embarrass my friend and boss, our team, and myself. Again. The shame and doubt I still carried from my spectacular failure weighed far too heavily to consider adding another failure to the list.

I told my boss what I was afraid of, and he burst out laughing.

"Danessa, you're not going to fail. I hired you because you are the only person who can get this right. The only way you'll fail is by not giving this your all. Get over yourself. If something goes wrong, I'll cover you. You've got this."

In less than a minute, we'd addressed and removed my interference. I trusted his assessment and trusted his word. I was safe and able to focus my full attention on the task at hand. Six months later, we'd delivered five times the revenue of our initial projections, and my failure was firmly behind me.

Sara and I didn't walk around looking ashamed. We wouldn't have called what we were feeling shame. Shame is a deeply painful, often very private negative emotion. Shame can masquerade as nearly any negative feeling. People harboring shame can look angry, anxious, or fearful. They can lash out at others or carry their burden more privately. Shame can show up as relentless drive or immeasurable caution.

Shame is different than its cousin, anger. Anger is loud and externally directed. Shame whispers and directs its focus inward. Shame is different than anxiety or fear; it is steadier, more permanent, and grows within. Shame is different than guilt. Guilt is about something you've done, a finite action separate from your identity. Shame is deeper; it is about who you are.

In 1998, Monica Lewinsky was twenty-five years old. She went to lunch with her friend Linda Tripp on a cold January afternoon, and soon after she sat down, two federal agents appeared. Monica learned then that her friend had been recording their conversations, and her secret affair with President Bill Clinton was no longer secret. The story was an instant worldwide spectacle. Monica was mercilessly shamed as details of the affair were made public, tapes of her conversations were released, and her clothing became evidence in a federal investigation.

"I felt like every layer of my skin and my identity were ripped off of me in '98 and '99," she said in 2016. "It's a skinning of sorts. You feel incredibly raw and frightened. But I also feel like the shame sticks to you like tar."

The story swallowed Lewinsky for twenty years. She couldn't find work, eat dinner out in public, or share details of her life online. The shame associated with her (mutual and consensual) affair with Clinton left her completely alone, belonging nowhere. Lewinsky names the exclusion of shame specifically, saying, "The fear of being ostracized strikes at the core of who we are. We cannot survive alone."

In 2015, Lewinsky chose to change the narrative. She began speaking out about her shame, telling her side of the story and what happened next, first in a *Vanity Fair* article titled "Shame and Survival" and then in a viral TED Talk. Today, Lewinsky is a vocal and respected anti-bullying advocate: "If I'm stuck with my past, giving it purpose feels meaningful to me."

Lewinsky's story reminds us of the steep cost of shame. The feeling of being judged not worthy of belonging, for an afternoon or a decade, is a powerful motivator. We work hard to avoid shame. We conceal parts of our pasts we consider shameful and avoid risk for fear of future shame.

Managing or avoiding shame at work can be all-consuming for leaders and teams. Regardless of how it shows up or whether it is real or imagined, shame is the strongest obstacle to a performer's effective inner game. In the coming chapters, we'll talk about what you can do to move past that obstacle and achieve your full leadership potential.

KEY TAKEAWAYS:

- "Shame" isn't a word we use often, and we don't like it.
- Shame is a negative feeling tied to identity; it tells us we are not enough.
- Shame can look and sound like anger, fear, anxiety, and other difficult emotions.
- You might be affected by shame and not be able to name it.

REFLECTION:

- When have you felt shame in the past?
- How did you address that shame? Did that help you or make things worse?
- Where might shame affect you today?

CHAPTER 4

Now What?

"If you want to know the taste of a pear, you must change the pear by eating it yourself. If you want to know the theory and methods of revolution, you must take part in revolution. All genuine knowledge originates in direct experience."

—MAO ZEDONG

You now understand that the path to leadership isn't straight or narrow. All types of leaders can be effective, drawing on their unique backgrounds. You understand that your performance is a function of your potential minus your interference, and that interference can be almost anything. You get that shame is a big deal; as Brené Brown says, "We're all walking around up to our eyeballs in it."

But if you're like many of my clients, you're wondering

why any of this matters. How can these case studies in a book help you in the real world? How can you step shamelessly forward into the leader you are meant to be, and your team is waiting for, by reading a handful of chapters?

Better said: now what?

Now it's time to act.

What you've learned so far is the foundation for a process that will change how you think about yourself and how you lead your team. This six-step transformation will enable you to tap into your courage, remove your interference, and power your performance and that of your organization.

The process I outline in the following chapters is the same work I do one-on-one over six months with my executive clients. Partnering closely, we combine leadership theory, examples, and opportunities to reflect with practice. We remove interference and drive performance. Leaders who do the work and follow the process see tremendous growth in themselves as leaders and in the results of their organizations.

The steps aren't easy; they take practice and repetition. But the process is simple, and like any simple task, you can begin working through it at once.

Here's what I'll show you over the next six chapters to lead your team with fearless authenticity:

1. Stop wasting your time on shame (chapter 5).
2. Take a good, hard look at where you are. And then embrace it (chapter 6).
3. Reframe or trash the stories you're telling yourself that don't serve you (chapter 7).
4. Mine your failures for golden gifts (chapter 8).
5. Get naked at work (the right way) (chapter 9).
6. Get it wrong. Recognize it's hard and do it again anyway (chapter 10).

Once you're clear on the process, we'll cover how to bring it forward to your team. Each of the following chapters will challenge how you think. You will unpack and rework years of how you've seen and done things. You're not alone; I'll guide you in the same way I work with my private clients. As in the previous chapters, you'll find stories, examples, opportunities to reflect on your experience, ways to practice new behaviors, and more. You can learn this. You can be a trusted beacon of authenticity in your organization. Let's get started.

CHAPTER 5

Stop Wasting Your Time on Shame

"Dogs have boundless enthusiasm but no sense of shame. I should have a dog as a life coach."

—MOBY

It was 2 a.m. I was elbow deep in baked ziti and completely and utterly overwhelmed. I was filling the pans with pasta, topping them with cheese and sauce, and adding the lid and label like a robot. It was certainly not where I wanted to be in the wee hours of that long-ago morning. But I didn't know what else to do.

This wasn't what I'd envisioned when I set out to build my Make-It-and-Take-It retail dinner store. In the early 2000s, I left my corporate job and wrote a plan for a business that helped busy families put home-cooked meals on the table. I found a partner and a loan and began to build out a retail space. Because I dare spectacularly, as my mother says, I'd jumped in with only a keen understanding of the pressures facing working parents, knowledge of the data supporting the importance of a family dinner, and a healthy dose of naivete. I'd never worked in food service and my retail experience was limited to an after-school job at a local Hallmark store. I also didn't cook, period. I once served Hot Pockets on plates with a side of peas and called it dinner.

Even so, the business opened successfully and grew rapidly. I did know how to hire and build teams and processes, and those skills served me well. I had a staff of fifteen working nearly full time prepping a dozen food stations a week with the ingredients for meals that froze well and cooked fast. Clients couldn't get enough of our product. For many busy women, leaving our store after two hours and a glass of wine with a dozen ready-to-cook meals for their family felt like nothing short of a miracle. Soon they brought their friends, and we'd launched a new kind of girls' night out.

After a feature article in the *Washington Post*, we blew past our first-year revenue projections. We began to look at a second location, and after watching the market and scouting property, we opened our second store within that first year.

I was living my dream. I didn't miss the safe corporate job (and paycheck) because I'd built something of my own. I had time to spend with my little boys, then four and one, and was still able to support my family as the primary breadwinner. I was helping parents, particularly working women, serve healthy dinners to their families with no guilt, and it was fun.

And then the economy collapsed.

As much as I tried to show our customers that meals made in our facility cost less than cooking at home (and they did), our sales began to dwindle. Customers considered premade meals a luxury to be eliminated when belts were tightened. For many, our $200 price tag didn't make the budget cut. They began to replace meals from our store with cheaper options, hot grocery store takeout and frozen food. The money that once flowed freely into our profit and loss statement was now being redirected to mortgages and credit card bills.

I had to cut my employees' hours, and I stopped taking a paycheck. We ramped up our grassroots marketing efforts and cut back on radio ads. I negotiated a plan with my banker to pay interest only on my loans, hoping to buy time until the tide turned. We missed a payment to our food supplier. It felt scary and overwhelming, but I told myself (and everyone else) that it was temporary.

I was confident it would get better, that I'd figure something out.

Until that night.

We'd gotten a big corporate order. The customer ordered 120 family-sized baked zitis for their employees to take home one Friday afternoon as a reward for meeting a monthly target. I didn't have the budget to pay the staff to complete the orders, but we couldn't turn away a sale that large. It felt like a windfall, and I began to fantasize about converting all those families to regular paying customers.

I decided to make the meals myself. We closed that day at six, and the order was scheduled for pickup at noon the following day. I boiled the first batch of pasta and told my husband I'd be home shortly after the boys went to bed.

Hours later, I understood that wasn't going to happen. I'd filled less than half the order, and I was exhausted. The dirty dishes were piled in the sink, and half-full pans of ziti were stacked all over the kitchen.

As I surveyed the mess, I suddenly saw it for what it was: a desperate and hopeless metaphor for the store. I wasn't going to finish this order, and this business wasn't going to survive. No matter how hard I worked or how much I wanted to save this night and my store, I was going to fail.

I was going to let down my young family and my employees. The weight of that realization was so overpowering it doubled me over. I could barely breathe. Years later, I can still feel the fear gnawing in the pit of my stomach.

Did I rally the troops, calling in my husband, friends, and employees to help me fill the endless stream of empty pans? Did I sit down with my banker and structure a plan to exit the business and cut my losses?

Excellent ideas, but I didn't have them. I did nothing. I was so overwhelmed by the shame about what I now understood was going to happen that I was immobilized. That night, I just kept filling ziti pans and tried to put it out of my mind. In the days that followed, I busied myself with small daily distractions, anything that kept me from having to face the big-picture reality of my situation.

My staff arrived to open the store in the morning and found me barely awake and still filling pans. "Why didn't you call us?" they asked, as they scrubbed in and took over. "We could've helped you." I didn't have an answer. It was the same question my banker asked six full months later when I finally told him how bad things had gotten. I still didn't know. I just couldn't.

I know now. Shame is paralyzing. I was so overwhelmed

by the idea of losing everything that I had no energy left to prevent it.

Working to manage or prevent shame sucks all resources. Never once in those months did I invest any real effort in figuring out what I could do to help myself and the business. I was too embarrassed to share the reality of my situation with anyone, so I didn't ask for help. I could see the end coming, and the fear and shame was so overwhelming I screwed my eyes shut and braced for impact. The black hole of shame swallows all energy. Aiming to reduce risk and avoid failure blocks maximizing success or pursuing innovation.

My example is not an anomaly. Bracing for impact is a hallmark of CYA (Cover Your Ass) cultures. Many companies today myopically focus on risk management and damage control to minimize exposure and the potential for error. Those efforts require time and energy that could be invested more powerfully.

Consider when you've been focused on preventing failure; did you achieve the best possible outcome? What's the innovation track record of companies who focus on minimizing risk? **No wild success has ever sprung from a company thinking small and safe.**

This isn't only true for leaders and organizations; it is

true for nearly every living organism from the simple cell to the blue whale. In repeated studies, scientists have found that living things can either defend themselves or grow. Think of a child fighting disease and being smaller than his classmates, or a plant fighting for space in a crowded garden and thus never bearing fruit. The farming industry has invested millions of research dollars and years of time into producing crops that can grow big and strong while also being pest- and drought-resistant. To date, genetic engineering has produced only one plant that can do both simultaneously, a modified strain of wheat.

When organisms, people, or teams focus on defense and survival, they cannot grow and thrive.

When I first understood what was ahead of me, the total and abject failure of my business, the looming shame paralyzed me. When I finally stepped away, after laying off staff and selling equipment, I thought I might be free of that awful feeling. But I was wrong.

Shame has an elephant's long memory. We remember failures and missteps forever, even if those events aren't always at the forefront of our minds. Quick, think about your biggest embarrassment in high school. Feels pretty clear and present, right? We pay the cost of shame in installments over time.

My client Mark, a young leader in a Fortune 50 company, worried about interacting with his C-suite executives. He'd been with the company about five years and had been promoted annually, a rate three times faster than any of his peers. He had a long list of internal sponsors and was often invited to networking events that involved spending time with the most senior leaders in the organization.

In his coaching session, Mark asked if we could focus our time on helping him prepare for an upcoming dinner.

"I don't want to look stupid again. I know the CEO will be there, and I want to look intelligent."

I was curious. Mark didn't need to *look* intelligent; he *is* intelligent. He has a proven track record of success. He has a strong leader presence about him and is typically very well spoken. I asked him to tell me more.

He explained that he sometimes had kind of an out-of-body experience when talking to senior leaders. He described it as floating above the conversation and watching it unfold. He would see himself talking to them and begin worrying about his word choice and what they might think after they left the conversation. When he returned to his body, his mind was blank. He'd stand with the leader, feeling terribly stupid and unable to move the conversation forward.

We dug deeper. Mark told me about the incident at the root of his worry. During a very difficult time for the company, the CEO approached Mark at a dinner and asked how he was feeling. Mark replied that his team was feeling positive, engaged, and ready to tackle the next obstacle.

"It was so stupid and out of touch," he said. "I looked like I had no sense of how challenging the circumstances were for the company. But I did—I just didn't articulate that."

Mark didn't get feedback from anyone listening that he was out of touch or looked naive. The CEO hadn't reacted negatively. He believed his ungrounded assessment about the conversation with the CEO, even without data. He hadn't considered the possibility that his comment might be viewed positively by his leadership. Knowing that his team was feeling strong and engaged during a tough period might have made the CEO feel great. But the assessment wasn't the only part of Mark's story to catch my attention. I also noticed its timeline: this conversation had happened a full *five years* earlier, when Mark had first joined the company.

For those five years, Mark had been watching himself in interactions with his leaders. After one infinitesimally small, arguably (at worst) neutral incident, he entered every conversation with senior leaders worrying that he'd look out of touch and stupid. He'd avoided opportunities to connect informally, sharing his observations and ideas and strengthening his reputation. He'd wasted five years on shame.

Shame's long memory goes hand in hand with a fixed mindset. A fixed mindset is the belief that you are or are not a certain way, you can or can't do something, or you do or do not have some characteristic. A fixed mindset doesn't allow for learning or change. It doesn't allow for evolution or correction. A growth mindset, on the other hand, allows for expansion and difference. It notices the same data but frames it differently.

I often have clients who tell me, "I'm not good at showcasing my work" or "I don't make good decisions under pressure." Those are fixed mindset statements. Consider those and compare them to these: "I haven't yet learned how to best showcase my work" or "I'm able to make good decisions, but pressure sometimes makes that more difficult." Do you see the difference?

The second statements are based on a growth mindset and assume that a positive outcome is possible. The first statements are fixed and don't allow for the possibility of correction. **Shame's fixed mindset ties our shortcomings to our identity, making them both more painful and more permanent. It whispers about what we are or aren't and doesn't leave room for what we might become.**

At this stage of the process, some of my clients claim that their shame serves them. They believe the fear of failure or compensating for earlier mistakes makes them perform better than their peers. Some view shame as the fuel to their fire and worry that neutralizing it may make them less effective.

Jennifer is the CEO of a large marketing company. Since founding her company nearly twenty years ago, she's grown her revenues significantly every year. She's a dynamic team builder and a proven leader. Her team and clients love the powerful combination of her charisma and focus on results.

Recently, in a hotel where she was attending a conference, she woke in the middle of the night with her heart racing. Worried she was having a heart attack, she called 911. Luckily, it was a false alarm, but the hospital's attending physician told her that she needed to slow down and rest.

Jennifer realized later that she didn't know how to follow his advice. Slow down? Rest? As long as she could remember, she'd been running. She didn't know how to stop.

Jennifer sifted through her experiences, looking back at her life to better understand when her engine started racing. Her answer? She had started running at breakneck speed in the first grade. *The first grade.*

Her teacher was primly traditional, a dusty relic from a different age. On the first day of school, she'd given her class of fresh-faced six-year-olds a placement test and drawn up the seating chart based on their scores.

"This row here, you are the smart ones. You in the middle, you're average. And you by the door? Well, you have work to do," Jennifer remembers her saying.

The rows were in order of the scores, and Jennifer was proud to be sitting in the first chair in the smart row. She'd earned the highest score in the class. She was determined to keep her position. Every time she took a test or turned in her homework, she thought about what it would feel like to move down. She now understands she spent the next forty years running to keep that seat.

The humiliating thought of moving her seat down fueled Jennifer's fire. Avoiding that shame drove significant, measurable success for her, but at a steep cost. She did not control that motivation, couldn't turn it on or off. She didn't draw upon the success of keeping the first-grade first-chair position as a source of fuel; she drew upon the fear of losing it. The story and the avoidance of shame controlled her rather than vice versa.

She's not alone. Many of my clients are very successful in part because they internalized a negative experience, or the mere idea of a negative experience, and allowed that to drive their future behavior. But that strategy often backfires. It creates a strong negative narrative and a fear of failure that prevents risk-taking. It creates interference for the leader and her team.

You may already be thinking the costs of shame are individual and private. No one knows how you feel, and it doesn't spill over to others. That's not true. Leaders who carry shame or work to prevent future shame can have a powerful negative effect on teams.

First, their focus is limited. Given a fixed number of hours in a day or capacity at work, a leader carrying shame must divide her time between managing that weight and managing her team.

Think managing shame doesn't take time? Think about the time Mark spent at the appetizer table trying to summon the courage to talk to the CEO. Now multiply that by five years. Because leaders direct the work of others, teams become entangled in managing shame. Think of the cost of Jennifer running at breakneck speed to achieve, and once she did, moving instantly to the next challenge. What might that feel like to a team? Have you ever been asked to write or rewrite a presentation to make it reflect better on a leader or team? That's the time suck of a leader's shame management.

Second, carrying shame inhibits innovation and creativity. Leaders who manage shame have their backs to the future and their focus firmly fixed on the past. They struggle to innovate or create because doing so means stepping into uncharted territory, risking failure and future shame. I see this often in groups who claim to want creativity, honest conversation, and innovation, but shoot down every idea on the whiteboard before the brainstorming session ends. Sound familiar? These leaders can't achieve the very growth they need because they are too focused on the potential downside of that risk. There's the "grow or defend" dilemma at the organizational scale.

Third, and finally, shame separates a leader from her team. That private weight creates a distance. She can connect but not fully. The connection is based on what she is willing to share publicly, not her whole and true self. Remember Emily, who returned to work after parental leave and wasn't comfortable talking about her new son? How connected could she really be to her team when she wasn't allowing that part of her through the office door? How connected was I to my team when I was too afraid to tell them the truth about what was happening to our store? Shame is a powerful barrier to authenticity.

If we extrapolate what we know about the effect of shame-focused leaders on teams to full organizations, we begin to see the full weight of this interference. Organizations that focus on avoiding shame struggle deeply with innovation, creativity, and culture. In these companies, teams are motivated not to lose rather than to win. There's no encouragement of wild ideas, no budget for what might initially feel like a flight of fancy.

Sometimes, failure is swept under the rug or politically spun to look and sound like something else. Sometimes, when teams fail, too much energy is poured into dissecting the failure for lessons learned. While that process sometimes drives innovation, teams often get stuck on what went wrong and avoid trying again. Organizations become siloed, political, and mired in the muck when the focus is on managing shame rather than reaching toward future potential.

Big tobacco companies offer a stark example of this dynamic. Understanding as early as the late 1950s that their product caused cancer, the leaders of those companies spent nearly fifty years pouring energy and resources into keeping this secret. They went as far as to fund studies with the specific purpose of muddying the scientific evidence of the connection between cigarettes and cancer. The focus was entirely on defense: defense of current revenue, defense of product, and defense of shame.

What if they'd invested that energy in developing a new, safe use for tobacco? What would have been possible?

Where might they be now? Probably not managing a $206 billion settlement agreement fund. Managing shame delivered nothing and had a very real cost.

The same thing can happen to full societies. In the United States, we manage collective shame about mental illness, drug and alcohol abuse, and the growing rate of death by suicide. These issues are rarely talked about in their full complexity because of the shame we individually and collectively manage around each. We struggle to bring them fully into the light and thus find them very difficult to solve.

In 2018, we saw what can happen when we get beyond shame and begin a conversation. The #MeToo movement, started by Tarana Burke in 2006, came to national prominence after the sexual abuse allegations against producer Harvey Weinstein. That viral hashtag thrust the issue of sexual harassment, especially in the workplace, into the global spotlight. Women and men who had been victims of sexual harassment and assault at work mustered the courage to come forward and speak openly about their experience. Together, the country began a united, productive conversation about the consequences and prevention of this behavior.

Certainly, we have not eradicated the problem or addressed the full extent of its reach. There are victims of harassment who still manage deep shame about what was done to them. I am confident, though, that in elevating the conversation, we have made it easier for victims to avoid the sinking black hole of shame. In doing so, we've empowered everyone from hotel maids to surgeons, actors to Air Force pilots, to focus wholly on their jobs. To use Gallwey's framework, we've removed a source of interference for millions of people. Think of what that means for our society. What's possible with so many people better able to reach their full potential?

The shame you carry isn't serving you. It is a source of interference that affects you and your team. You can choose not to invest your energy in managing shame from your past or preventing future shame. Stop wasting your time on shame and move forward toward your full potential.

Activist and writer Glennon Doyle says, "Shame is so self-indulgent and power-zapping. It leaves us useless. To ourselves, to our people, to the world. Self-flagellation is not a badge of honor. It doesn't make us worthy; it just makes us—kind of a drag. And it takes us out of the game. Who has time? What are we doing here, if not learning and growing and trying again? Why can't we do that with some lightness and tenderness and humor? Who we were last year, last hour, last minute—it's gone. We are new! Let us begin again!"

- Shame is a waste of time: it is paralyzing, backward-looking, and unproductive.
- Shame takes energy to maintain, and energy is a limited resource.
- Shame has a fixed mindset. A fixed mindset believes we are what we are with no options to shift. A growth mindset, on the other hand, believes we can evolve and change as the situation merits.
- While motivation is sometimes a benefit of carrying shame, the costs far outweigh the upside. Shame has no purpose.
- Shame prevents authenticity.
- Shame doesn't only affect its carrier; it has a ripple effect through teams.
- Shame creates disconnection, paralyzing organizations.
- When we neutralize shame, big things can happen for people, teams, and, sometimes, full societies.

REFLECTION:

- When has your shame served you?
- When have you noticed your mindset is fixed (I am..., I am not...)?
- How can you use the words "yet" and "up until now" to shift your mindset on what you believe to be true about yourself?

· **When have you seen the ripple effect of shame?**

CHAPTER 6

You Are Here.
Embrace It.

"Your present circumstances don't determine where you can go; they merely determine where you start."

—NIDO QUBEIN

"I should've done it differently," Kate tells me. "I should've delegated it earlier. I'm not good at delegating, and I didn't explain what I needed. I should've looked for ways to divvy up the task and give it to others. I should've thought more about what the team needed to achieve in the session. I should've shared our priorities."

She goes on, listing what feels like dozens of things she believes she could and should have done to avoid the predicament she is currently in. The only problem is, she's answering the wrong question. I haven't asked what she should've done. I've asked what she is planning to do.

Kate is the succession candidate for the chief human resource officer (CHRO) role at a Fortune 100 retail company. She is experienced, is quick on her feet, and cares deeply about people and talent. And on this day, she is facing some powerful interference.

Kate is stuck where many of us get stuck: in the land of "should." She delegated an important meeting to a subordinate while she was out of the office. That woman is a high potential star in Kate's organization. Kate briefly shared what she hoped to achieve in the meeting and went on vacation. She's returned to the office to find that the subordinate delegated the meeting to someone else. It happened but was a disaster—no agenda, rambling arguments, and nothing accomplished. Kate must clean up this mess today, or the project she's leading will derail too. She's now seeing how she contributed to the current predicament, and she's stuck on what went wrong.

Capturing lessons learned or ideas for next time solidifies learning and harnesses opportunity. Although it can be helpful, today it's getting in Kate's way.

It's hard to name lessons learned and move forward fast at work. We can too often intertwine our identity with what we do, and when we can see what we could have done differently, it feels uncomfortable. We slide into thinking about what we should have done and why we didn't, and invest time where it won't deliver a return. That time would be better invested thinking about how we're going to solve the problem instead of swirling in "shoulds."

Imagine driving in an unfamiliar place without a GPS. You pull over at a rest stop to study a large map posted on the wall. What's the first thing you look for?

You look for the You Are Here marker, not for where you want to be, nor at where you should've gone. You don't look at the path you've traveled. You look first for where you are.

Once you know where you are, you can effectively navigate to where you want to be. Once you understand your current position, you don't look at where you thought you were or how you got here with anything more than passing curiosity; those data points don't serve you. Dwelling on where you thought you were or how you got to this spot doesn't help much when you're lost. **You need to see accurately where you are and work out how to get from there to where you want to be.**

During the initial height of the #MeToo movement, I had

dinner with the CEO of a large professional services company. She was new to the role, moving into it after her predecessor and several other senior leaders were fired over charges of mishandling and covering up harassment claims. I asked her how she was approaching leading the team during such a challenging time.

"I've just had to be really honest about where we are," she said. "I don't have the energy or credibility to deliver a shiny spin on this. We're in a really tough place. Things are bad for us and for our former leaders. We've broken our employees' and customers' trust. I think we can make it through, but it's not going to be easy. We're staring this in the face and focused on moving past it one step at a time."

She wasn't confident or particularly positive. But she was honest, and it worked. Two years later, the firm had rebounded, winning large national contracts and a slew of industry awards. Her clear focus on where the team was and the challenge ahead, rather than what should have been, drove much of that success. Her clear-eyed view of the future combined with an honest assessment of where the company stood built her credibility. It allowed the team to concentrate attention and energy on what came next and reduced the conflict and swirl that can surface when companies dwell in what could or should have been done in the past.

Some leaders aren't overly focused on what should have been but rather are overly optimistic about how things are or might be in the future. This is another way to distort your view of the current state. These leaders avoid realistically assessing their situation by wearing rose-colored glasses. I see this in leaders who tell me they aren't actively managing a difficult team member because they believe he'll "get the message and self-correct" or she's "not *always* at the root of office drama."

I also see this happen in teams who've built strategies reliant on products or marketplace behaviors that are irrelevant or past their prime. This was the root of the demise of Blockbuster Video and at play now in every retail boardroom where leaders aren't talking about how to compete with Amazon. These leaders rely on hope as a strategy and struggle with the truth about where they and their companies actually are.

In his book *The Hard Thing About Hard Things*, Ben Horowitz recounts his days as CEO at Loudcloud and describes how close and often the company came to shutting its doors. Loudcloud, a managed-services software company, started as a darling of the tech world, valued at $66 million at sixty days old. In a race to market, Horowitz hired and spent aggressively. Loudcloud burned through three capital raises and began to miss revenue targets. Suddenly, there was no more private funding to be found.

Horowitz was continually three weeks away from shutting the doors. His unwavering focus on that "horrifying" possibility helped him turn the ship. He didn't indulge in fantasy or stick his head in the sand; he accurately assessed where they were.

That clear assessment drove his activity every waking hour. It fueled his idea to take the company public, a concept his board found borderline ridiculous, given the circumstances. The resulting press was scathing: *Businessweek* declared Loudcloud "the IPO from hell" and one analyst suggested the company had lost nearly $1 million per employee in the last year. Horowitz kept working the problem, driven by his brutally realistic perspective of the catastrophic alternative. He ultimately prevailed, raising a near-miraculous $162.5 million in an IPO timed exactly at the height of the dot-com crash. Unwavering focus on where you actually are and what must happen next to move forward produces results.

Back in my office, Kate is still naming all the ways she went wrong. I interrupt her long list of shoulds and walk her through the You Are Here map analogy. She is silent. After a long pause, she looks at me and says, "I'd like that printed on a large, blinking sign and hung above my desk, please."

Kate and I shift our focus to accurately assessing the current situation and what she must do to fix the problem. She moves forward fast. In our future sessions, she can more easily name where she is and where she wants to be. She no longer gets stuck on how she got here; she's entirely focused on what's next.

I use a variety of tools to help clients stop the should swirl and think objectively about where they actually are. For clients facing a challenging situation, like Kate, I use a variation of a SWOT analysis.

SWOT ANALYSIS

Brainstorm the strengths inherent to the team working the challenge, the internal weaknesses limiting performance, the opportunities the challenge presents, and the external threats to success. **Ask:** What do we do well? What are our unique capabilities? What obstacles do we face? What resources are limited? What's possible if we get this right? What's the best-case scenario? What if others beat us to market? Where might we be surprised by competitors? **Consider** possibilities for action. **Vet** with a larger team and **act**.

SWOT (strengths, weaknesses, opportunities, and threats) is usually used as a strategic planning framework. In my work, I use it as a pin-dropping tool on the organizational map. When clients are facing a challenge, I encourage them to list the strengths inherent to the team working the challenge, the weaknesses limiting performance, the opportunities the challenge presents, and the external threats to success. Once those components are on paper, we consider the possible options for action, vet those with a broader team, and move forward. SWOT analysis is especially helpful when clients are facing a specific challenge or decision point.

Often, though, interference with an accurate You Are Here assessment isn't a specific external obstacle. Instead, it can be unconscious behavior, a recurring pattern or point of view. It may be a narrative the leader holds about himself. Maybe it is about long-held values or patterns of behavior that no longer serve her or don't apply to that situation. In other words, sometimes what gets in the way of an accurate assessment is the leader's own self-awareness. When that's the case, I use a tool I call the Minute Manifesto to help a leader clarify her own assessment of herself.

Early in my career with a large Fortune 100 financial services firm, I was lucky enough to be offered two very different leadership roles. Because I love to dwell in possibility, I was having a hard time choosing between the two. I couldn't decide which would interest me more, drive the most learning, or offer the strongest future opportunity. I was waffling badly, and it was costing the business time and costing me credibility.

A mentor took me into a conference room with walls covered in whiteboards. He handed me a marker and motioned to the largest board.

"Who are you?" he asked. I stood there. "Who are you?" he repeated.

I answered hesitantly: "A manager?"

"Start writing. Write all the answers you have to that question until I tell you to stop. Who are you?"

So I wrote. I wrote "manager, wife, daughter, sister, volunteer cheerleading coach, active alumna, child of a diplomat, sixth-generation Californian, starter of projects." I wrote and wrote. Five full minutes passed, and he spoke again.

"What have you done? Same rules as before. Write all the things you've done up until now until I ask you another question."

I began again. I'd built the prototype for a new kind of call center service agent, graduated in the top 10 percent of my class, moved eighteen times, nearly failed organic chemistry and withdrawn, and quit every job I found tedious and repetitive without a second thought. Again, I wrote until he asked the next question.

"What do you believe in? Go."

Then, "What do you stand for?"

Finally, "How are you uniquely qualified to contribute?"

I'd covered every whiteboard in the room and moved to the legal pad I'd carried into the meeting. We were less than half an hour into our hour-long meeting, but he got up to leave.

"Look at what you wrote. Cut it in half. Then cut what's left in half. Then copy it down and take it to someone you trust. Ask them what's most true and what's missing. Edit it one final time. When you're done, you should be able to answer these questions in less than two minutes. And you'll know what job you want." He walked out.

He was right. I worked for the next two days on what I would come to call my personal manifesto, synthesizing it to one concise statement.

"I am a champion of people and a builder of new things. I've led teams large and small and been successful when the work is new and exciting. I swing for the fences, and I don't much care for small details or repetitive tasks. I stand for compassion and candor and believe that everyone can contribute. I can build engaged, powerful teams and rally them behind new concepts when I believe those teams and concepts will change things for the better."

I made my decision. The insight I gained from the work

I did over those two days has powered my progress for the past twenty years. When I am not sure what's next or unable to decide, I turn back to that statement. I've evolved and edited it over the years and continue to use the process and its output as a compass.

MINUTE MANIFESTO

For each of the following questions, handwrite or type your answers. Write continuously for five full minutes on each, and do not edit as you write. Represent yourself accurately—don't sugarcoat or be overly critical. This is for your eyes only at this point.

1. Who are you?

2. What have you done?

3. What do you believe in?

4. What do you stand for?

5. How are you uniquely qualified to contribute?

Wait at least one full day, and then edit what you've written. Remove anything that doesn't feel fully authentic, striving to reduce the content by half. Repeat after waiting at least one more full day.

Share your results with a trusted advisor, and ask them to be objective in their assessment of you. Edit once more based on their feedback.

Synthesize what's left into a succinct statement about yourself.

I now use this Minute Manifesto process with my clients. I don't bark at them in empty conference rooms; rather, I invite them to reflect on those questions independently. The parameters are the same: five minutes for each question; write continuously; edit the final product twice alone, then share it with a trusted confidant and edit again. The work yields powerful results and allows leaders to gain crisp new self-awareness as they consider what's next.

I also use two other exercises to help clients looking for an accurate internal assessment of their talents and achievements.

The first is the High-Low Career Map. To build a career map, take a piece of paper or two. Orient it to the landscape position and draw a horizontal line through the middle. Now, starting with your first job (and we're putting them all on here, so leave room or add a page), write it in a bubble above or below the line. If you loved it, write it far above. If you couldn't wait to leave, drop it to the bottom of the page. If you're able, jot a note or two about why it was high or low. Move fast—at most, you should spend fifteen minutes building the map.

Once you've plotted your jobs, step back and see what you notice. What do the highs have in common? The lows? Think both specifically and abstractly. Did you like what you did day to day in each of the highs? Did you work with people? Was the work tactical or theoretical? Were you at a desk or in the field? Where you were living then? What else was happening for you personally? Look for patterns within and beyond the work.

HIGH-LOW CAREER MAP

- Draw a horizontal line across the middle of a large piece of paper oriented to the landscape position.

- Moving quickly, plot each job you have held on the line. Place jobs you enjoyed above the line, and jobs you didn't below. Positions you loved should be placed higher than ones you liked, ones you hated lower than ones you simply tolerated. Note your rationale for placement in a word or two by each bullet.

- Step back and look for commonalities in jobs you enjoyed and jobs you didn't. Consider both the actual elements of the jobs as well as less obvious similarities.

- Capture what you've learned.

The High-Low Career Map helps you understand what your experience has been up until now and how you felt about it. You can then mine it for ways to recreate when you've felt your best and explore new possibilities for action.

The second exercise is the Proud Personal History. Think first of a person you love, someone who you can unabashedly brag about yourself to. For some, this is a grandmother or a mom, maybe a favorite uncle. I've even had clients choose their horse or dog! Write that person a letter that details each proud moment of your life, whether or not it was related to work. The list can be long—if it made you proud, even secretly, it's in.

The second step is the same as for the High-Low Career Map. Step back and look for patterns. Notice what you felt when you were forced to think only of what you were proud of. Was it easy? Hard? What were the inner gremlins whispering?

Those gremlins love to whisper, "You can't be proud of that; it didn't last," "It would've been even better if..." and "That's not worth being proud of." Don't listen. The goal in each of these exercises is to avoid self-indulgence—good or bad. We're not breaking our arm patting ourselves on the back nor whipping ourselves into shape. We're simply aiming for a complete picture to help form an accurate assessment.

PROUD PERSONAL HISTORY

1. Write a letter to your biggest fan detailing everything that has happened to you that has made you proud.

2. Don't edit; if it made you proud, it goes on the list.

3. Look for similarities between the events. Consider both the actual circumstances as well as less obvious themes that might emerge.

4. Capture what you've learned.

Once clients have completed one or more of these exercises, they have a solid sense of where they and their teams are. The You Are Here pin is on the map.

Swirling about what you think you should have done or avoiding reality doesn't serve you and burns energy. Accurately assess your current state objectively. With the exercises in this chapter, I have helped many leaders better understand their own unique capabilities and their team's current position. Sometimes, simply knowing where you are allows you to move quickly to the next great success.

Often, though, the You Are Here pin seems very far from where you want to be. Sometimes it can feel like you've wound up at the end of a long string of stories that should have gone differently. Sometimes, it can feel like creating new self-awareness only highlights all the ways you're wrong for this job and this challenge. And that's exactly what we address in the next chapter.

KEY TAKEAWAYS:

· **Leaders can lose sight of where they and their teams are, deliberately or by accident.**
· **Progress toward a goal isn't possible without knowing your starting point.**
· **Understanding your current unique position is a**

better use of your time than focusing on where you think you should be.

- Exercises can help you step back and assess where you and the team are.

REFLECTION:

- When have you focused on where you thought you should be rather than where you were? How did that serve you?
- When have you wanted to believe something that wasn't true about your work?
- What does it feel like to focus forward on progress rather than back at the gap?

PRACTICE:

Choose two of the exercises outlined in this chapter (and below) to practice forming an accurate assessment of your current state.

- SWOT
- Minute Manifesto
- High-Low Career Map
- Proud Personal History

CHAPTER 7

Rewrite Your Stories

"You are your own stories."

—TONI MORRISON

Across from me sits Nicholas, tall and lanky, leaning back comfortably with his legs crossed. His hair is slightly longer than you might expect of a high-powered venture capital investor, but his suit is carefully and expensively tailored. He's classically handsome and smiles easily, making you think he's the kind of man who was elected prom king and senior class president in high school, the kind of man who is cozily familiar with success.

And, in fact, Nicholas is very successful. He's young and accomplished, and up for a significant promotion at work. Before he built his investment career, he won an Olympic medal in a sport he loves. He's married, with two young sons. On paper, he checks all the boxes.

His reality is different.

I've been hired to help Nicholas secure his promotion. He's in a fast-paced, up-or-out culture, and this is his last chance. He's failed the process before because his senior leaders find him too abrasive; he's not the culture beacon they expect senior leaders to be. He appears insensitive to the needs and concerns of others, doggedly focusing on the task at hand. He understands what they've told him and can sometimes see the behaviors they've called out, but he can't figure out how to stop. Today, we're talking about what drives that singular focus.

"I'm not sure where it comes from," Nicholas begins. "I think it's because I'm the youngest of three brothers, and I've always been racing to keep up."

Nicholas tells me that his brothers graduated at the top of their classes from Ivy League colleges. He went to an outstanding public institution, but it wasn't an Ivy. His brothers went on to law school and are now successful attorneys being eyed for the next open positions on the bench in their communities. This is a path Nicholas's family knows well; his father is also a judge who went to an Ivy League university.

"When I go home for the holidays, no one is impressed by what I do. No one even understands it," he says.

Nicholas's Olympic silver medal is a source of both pride and frustration. He's not alone. Silver medalists are often the least satisfied winners on the podium; it's not easy to come so close to being the best. Psychologists Victoria Medvec and Thomas Gilovich of Cornell University, with Scott Madey of the University of Toledo, quantified this in a 1992 study of the Barcelona Olympics. The team showed footage of the event, the moments immediately following the event, and the medal ceremony to undergraduate students. They asked the students to rate the visible happiness of the medal winners on a scale of 1 to 10. One was described as agony, 10 as ecstasy. Immediately after the event, the silver medalists scored a 4.8, and the bronze medalists scored a 7.1. At the medal ceremony, the silver medalists scored a 4.3 and the bronze medalists scored 5.7. In both instances, bronze medalists, the people who just made it to the podium, were visibly happier than their silver counterparts, who'd recently learned they were best in the world except for one person.

"I've always had to work to win," Nicholas says. "I'm not the smartest guy in the room, but I'll fight hardest."

Nicholas is telling himself a powerful story. In his mind, he's the underdog, the dark horse unlikely to take the prize. Again and again, he's fought against others to stand out; first against his brothers, then his fellow Olympians, now his colleagues. That fighter mentality served him to an extent, but it is limiting him now.

The senior leadership team at his firm already knew he could win individually; they wondered if he could lead a team. To be promoted, Nicholas had to stop fighting. He was now being evaluated for his ability to collaborate and inspire followership, not his ability to compete. Nicholas had to tell himself a new story; the old one was driving the wrong behavior and getting in his way.

Humans make meaning of experience by stringing events together to tell a story. Dan McAdams, a Northwestern University psychology professor who has studied life stories his full career, describes our very identity as "the internalized and evolving story that results from a person's selective appropriation of past, present, and future." That selective appropriation of events is the key to understanding the power of reframing story.

Reframing looks at the facts you know and assessments you hold about a subject and objectively considers what conclusions you might draw *in addition to* the one you have believed up until now. It is asking, "And what else?" It is a powerful practice, opening possibility and creativity.

Most of us carry secret stories about ourselves and others. We repeat them to ourselves so often that we begin to believe them as objective truth. But they aren't. They're still stories, no matter how often we tell them or how confidently we believe them. They are simply how we've made meaning of our own unique experiences. We often don't have a clear idea of the stories we tell ourselves or the power they hold until we look at them closely, understand the events we have selected, and consider how those selected events shaped our perspective and beliefs.

I have a simple example I share to help clients see how early and easily we adopt a story about ourselves and what's possible when we reframe it. For much of my adult life, I believed that I wasn't an athlete. I shied away from team sports and was more comfortable sitting on my couch with a book than in any endeavor that involved a ball.

This belief started early, much to the chagrin of my sports-loving father. When I was six, I was given a matching worksheet in school; I had to draw a line between the soccer ball and the cleat, the football helmet and the football, the hockey stick and the puck, and so on. I failed it miserably.

Five years later, I was standing on third base in the sunshine, looking closely at the spring grass around my feet for a four-leaf clover. Kickball didn't hold my interest. Suddenly, I heard someone shouting, "Run!" It was Richard Howard, my sixth-grade crush, bearing down on me after having kicked the ball well outside of the home run boundaries. We lost the game because I was too flustered to move, and apparently when one player passes another on the bases the lapper is out.

The years passed and I never touched the bat and ball Santa optimistically left under the tree for me. By the time I was in high school, mistakenly calling track practice rehearsal, I'd written my story as an uncoordinated anti-jock in stone.

It was only when I learned about the power of reframing stories that I started to reconsider the data I'd seen as irrefutable. That test I failed when I was six? Up until then, I'd lived overseas, in South Africa and the Dominican Republic. I'd moved back to the US only thirty days before, and I had never seen many of those items, let alone the associated sports. While I wasn't interested in kickball when I was eleven, I was a strong swimmer, and I set and held the high-jump record in my middle school. I danced for most of my childhood, and my long, lanky build helped me power a mean volleyball serve. Sprinkled between the failures I remembered were an equal number of successes.

I believed a story that I started telling myself when I was six. I had other information to consider, but I chose one set of data early. As I grew, I unconsciously chose to include experiences that cemented that story and ignore ones that might have refuted it. Researchers call that a "reflective loop." When we believe something to be true, and we select only data that reinforces that perspective, it strengthens the belief and makes us more likely to choose data aligned to it in the future. This cycle of see-believe-reinforce fixes narratives over time and narrows our choices for action. Why watch the BBC when CNN is already on?

When I looked closely at the story and began to include the other data I had, a new picture emerged. I don't like to try new things in front of lots of people (does anyone?). I'm not driven by competition. That might be what I find less appealing about team sports, but it doesn't mean I'm not able or athletic. Reframing the story to say that I am able and have preferences about how I exercise my body allowed me to train for and complete a half marathon.

When I work with clients to reframe stories, I first encourage them to understand how the story they're currently telling both helps and hinders them. Usually, clients believe a story does one of the two, but **all stories both serve and limit us.** When I told myself the story of the uncoordinated anti-jock, I was limited in my ability to exercise my body, try new experiences, and compete with others. I was served by that story because I didn't have to risk embarrassment or exposure or try to compete to be good, and I had a convenient excuse to not exercise. I could stay in the stands at sporting events eating Cracker Jack rather than fielding the ball. I was both served and limited.

Nicholas was served by his underdog story because that drove him to try harder than anyone else and he credited his wins to that effort. He was also limited, because if you're always competing, you don't collaborate. Served and limited.

We also examine who's telling the current story. Nicholas's story was told by a very young little brother. A six-year-old girl told my story. Those early versions of ourselves aren't very trustworthy. Six-year-olds don't see the world in the same way adults do. Once a story takes hold, that early version of ourselves starts looking for information to confirm her beliefs. We all carry stories about ourselves told by our earlier versions that don't have the full breadth and depth of our current knowledge and experience. Yet we believe them.

As we examine our stories and ourselves as storytellers, it's important to separate our critique of the story from criticism of ourselves. We can hold the story out in front of us and objectively examine it without tearing down the storyteller. The earlier version of ourselves that spun that story wasn't working against us; she was making meaning of the world as she understood it. We can be wildly generous to our earlier selves. As the speaker Jenny Patinkin says, "I have some issues with my past self, but she was young, and I forgive her."

A methodology I often share with clients working to reframe a story is Hero in Victory or Retreat. Professor Neil Stroul introduced me to this framework on my first day of the executive coaching program at Georgetown University. I've since encountered it several times, and it continues to be a powerful tool for reframing stories we carry.

We are all the heroes in our own stories—not the hero like Superman or one of the Marvel Universe buff bodies but the protagonist of the story (think Odysseus). The Hero in Victory or Retreat framework focuses on how we respond to circumstance.

When we are in victory, we show up as our best selves. We are a hero in victory when we feel alive, energized, and as though we are fully capturing our potential. We are proud of ourselves and our achievements and aware of our unique gifts. When we are in retreat, we are driven by the negative gremlins in our heads. We worry about scarcity, focus on past mistakes, and see how far a distance there is between where we are and where we want to be.

The framework allows us to move between perspectives using the same situation or circumstances. You can choose to view any situation in your past from the perspective of a hero in victory or that of a hero in retreat. Think of the Wicked Witch of the West from *The Wizard of Oz*. When we watch the Technicolor movie, we think of her as pure evil, shuddering when she unleashes her flying monkeys and cheering as she melts. Watching *Wicked* on stage, we have a very different view of Elphaba. We appreciate her sense of humor and believe that, as a spinoff novel suggests, Dorothy must die. By opening ourselves up to other possible interpretations of events, we can explore a new perspective.

The hero framework allows you to change hats in your familiar stories. When you are feeling small or less than your peers and deep in a negative narrative, you can thank the hero in retreat for her perspective and ask her to sit down. You can ask, "What might this same situation look like through my hero in victory eyes?" Yes, it feels artificial and awkward. And it works. Calling forward your Hero in Victory to share her view can help balance your perspective. A balanced perspective and careful evaluation of your story is the first step to reframing it. **Two heroes exist in every circumstance; which you call forward is entirely up to you.**

Sometimes, as I explain the hero's framework, I see clients begin to distance themselves. Their eyes glaze and they move back a bit in their seat, nodding politely, sometimes adding, "Interesting," for good measure. Their words don't matter. Their body language makes clear that this framework, this choosing your own hero and adventure silliness, doesn't land for them. It feels artificial and a bit self-help-y, if they were to be honest. I appreciate that. Reframing can seem artificial and manufactured.

But the truth is, if we are working through a story in coaching, that story is interfering with their performance. It is what's in the way of them being the authentic, successful leader they can be. When I am sitting in front of a client, they are working to change a behavior, and in order to change that behavior, they must begin to think differently. The framework does this, giving a new look at old stories and making us think differently about the circumstances that shaped us.

Here's the same challenge I give to my most skeptical clients: try the Hero in Victory or Retreat framework on one of your most pervasive negative stories. Commit to the full process: talk through the story as you know it now, think about it in a new way, wonder about how you got to the conclusion you did, and consider what version of yourself drew that conclusion. Explore how you might think about it if you switched your hero from retreat to victory. You don't have to believe it. Just consider what might be possible if you did. What if you carried a new version of that story around, instead of the shitty, banged-up one you made up? Because you did make it up. Remember, real facts are few. Your stories are largely a string of assessments.

David was one of my most skeptical clients, working as the COO in a small national nonprofit in a large metropolitan area. He had seen himself as the underdog his full career—fighting the good fight against insurmountable odds again and again and again. He passionately believed in the mission of his organization and defended it fiercely each time it was threatened. And it was threatened often: insecure funding, fluctuating national support, and difficult staffing. The walls were always closing in, and David was always ready to fight.

David fought the underdog fight at home too. He'd grown up gay in a deeply conservative religious family and struggled to reconcile his beliefs with his upbringing. He was sensitive to other underdogs and was an energetic supporter of social justice causes. And he carried all that baggage.

David carried the full weight of every fight he ever lost. He reviewed over and over what he might have done differently, combing those experiences for evidence of where he went wrong. What if he'd applied for another grant? Had he unintentionally offended his coworkers by deprioritizing their initiatives? How could the organization have lost the support of that donor?

Underdog David made himself the loss historian, reviewing every missed opportunity and hopeless cause. This endless review left him little energy to develop and execute a vision for the organization. The fear he might repeat an old mistake or make a new one nearly paralyzed him.

As we worked to reframe his story, David realized he wasn't bound to carry the weight of all the losses up until now. He'd been doing so to honor his efforts and those of other justice fighters. But that habit no longer served him. It no longer revved up his fury and energized him as it had in the past. In fact, it did the opposite. It exhausted and overwhelmed him, sapping his energy and dragging him down.

David took a new look at his approach and decided he would leave the baggage on the platform. Rather than carry the weight of his missteps, he would face what he perceived as the risk of forgetting them. He changed his story from the keeper of losses and history to the future-focused leader. This new story energized and powered him forward. It served him.

David didn't change his circumstances; he changed his

thinking from retreat to victory. And he was better for it, as was his team and social circle. The approach felt artificial at first. He asked me incredulously, "You mean I should just forget all this?" But he soon understood that it was as honest and true a story as his first, and more effective.

This "fake it 'til you make it" or "will what you want to be true" tactic is often judged as disingenuous. It can be dismissed as overly woo-woo or touchy-feely. But what we believe to be true, about ourselves especially, often is. Don't like who you are? Tell yourself a different story and believe it.

Pete Best is a classic example of this. Best was the original drummer for the Beatles and played on their demo album. Many considered him to be the most charming and handsome of the group. Best was talented and also had a strong head for business. But in the weeks before the demo took off, the band fired him. He was out. Best watched his former bandmates' meteoric rise to fame and fortune and lived his life in their shadow.

Years later, this story repeated for Dave Mustaine, the first lead guitarist for Metallica. Days before Metallica's demo launched and started the band on the road to stardom, Mustaine was roused from a doped-up slumber, fired, and given a bus ticket home.

Two talented musicians ousted from their bands right before each hit it big. Big being an understatement. The Beatles became, well, the Beatles, and Metallica became the biggest metal band of all time. But that's where the similarities between the Pete Best and Dave Mustaine stories end.

Mustaine went on to form the thrash-metal band Megadeth, selling 38 million albums worldwide, winning twelve Grammys, and seeing six of fifteen albums go platinum. He played sold-out stadiums all over the world and changed the face of heavy metal music. Megadeth is considered one of the most musically influential groups of the 1980s. Still, he spent that time chasing Metallica. In interviews as many as thirty-five years later, Dave is focused on his expulsion from the band and still considers himself less than his former bandmates. He is angry and inflammatory. In the story he tells himself, his success is far overshadowed by his perceived failure. He is a hero in retreat.

Pete Best, on the other hand, lived a quiet, happy life. He continued to play drums simply for the love of it and wasn't forced to cater to changing musical tastes or producers' whimsy. He met and married the love of his life, something he said he's sure wouldn't have happened if he'd been partying his way around the world. He lived in a small town, where he had genuine friendships that he believes might never have taken root if he'd been a megastar. He was a present father to his two daughters and is a fan of his former band's music. Best chose his hero in victory and believed the best version of his story. And that made all the difference.

HOW TO REFRAME YOUR STORY

1. Look carefully at the story you're telling and notice how it both serves and limits you.

2. Consider what earlier version of yourself is telling the story. Which hero leads?

3. Find ways to look at the data differently or add new information. What might your other hero see?

4. Reframe the story to reflect the new data and possibility.

5. Tell yourself the new story as often as you did the old and believe the better version.

I use the stories of Mustaine and Best often with clients to illustrate the power of reframing. When Nicholas heard them for the first time, he thought I was preparing him for his own version of being tossed out of a band: not getting his promotion.

Always the scrappy fighter, he responded, "That's bullshit. I deserve that promotion, and I'm going to win it." That's exactly the thinking we worked to reframe. Nicholas's story of himself as the underdog, always having to work to win, cast the promotion process as a competition with a simple win/lose outcome. We worked to reframe Nicholas's work and the promotion process as less of an individual competition and more of a team sport, where winning meant collaborating with teammates and leading subordinates effectively.

Over time, Nicholas shifted his focus from proving he was better than others as an individual performer to proving his ability to build and lead teams that could replicate his strong results. Lots changed during this time. He began seeing mentorship differently, for example. He no longer viewed it as taking time away from his work but as a critical priority. He was open to networking and supporting others in new ways because he saw value in that investment. Conversations with colleagues built connections, not his prowess. Reframing his definition of winning allowed Nicholas to strengthen his relationships and develop his emotional intelligence. And those two factors drove his promotion. Nicholas changed his thinking and changed his reality.

Reframing is a simple process to explain. Think about what story you're telling and how it both serves and limits you. What version of you first told that story? What's changed? Explore what other available information might, if incorporated into your narrative, tell a different story. Simple to explain and hard to do. Telling yourself a new story is difficult because it requires repeated practice and conscious intention. With practice, you can reframe the old stories that limit you into new ones that inspire and serve you.

At this point, clients often look at me and say, "Clearly, you don't know my story about..." and describe a spectacular failure from their past. Leaders often struggle most with reframing stories about failure. Total and abject failure can feel like a negative story that's impossible to rewrite. We'll tackle that tough topic in the next chapter.

KEY TAKEAWAYS:

- **Our assessments of ourselves and our surroundings are stories that we tell ourselves.**
- **Over time, those stories can feel like reality.**
- **You can reframe your stories to see new data and make new choices.**
- **Reframing is an active habit:**
  - **Look carefully at the story you're telling.**
  - **Understand how it both serves and limits you.**
  - **Consider what earlier version of yourself is telling the story.**
  - **Explore ways to look at data differently or add new data.**
  - **Reframe the story to reflect the new data and possibility. (Consider your hero.)**

- What you believe is what will be; you have a clear choice.

REFLECTION:

- In tough circumstances, when has your best self emerged?
- How does it feel when you are in retreat? In victory?
- How might you begin to reframe a story about your past?

CHAPTER 8

The F Word

"Whatever causes night in our souls may leave stars."

—VICTOR HUGO

I can still remember seeing Mr. Ehrlich leap to his feet in a desperate attempt to help me even as it became obvious the situation was hopeless. That is my clearest memory of the precise moment I realized I was in a failure freefall.

The first time I failed spectacularly I was sixteen years old, and a junior in my high school's chorus. We were practicing for a big production, a compilation of songs from musicals performed while the audience nibbled on a smorgasbord of sweets. The revue, aptly named *Dessert on Broadway*, was a Very Big Deal. This was in the years before YouTube and DirecTV, and entertainment options were limited. In my sleepy suburb, *Dessert on Broadway* was a tradition, and nearly three hundred people came each of the three nights we performed the show in the high school cafeteria.

We'd been planning and practicing the show for months. At sixteen, and fully self-involved, I wanted to be at my best. My song, "I'm Gonna Wash That Man Right Outa My Hair," was memorable enough, but the staging involved washing my hair in a bucket and harmonizing with my friend Jo, a much better singer. The logistics of onstage shampoo mixed with the very real possibility of being outsung meant a change had to be made. I was sixteen, after all. I still believed the world revolved around me.

I wheedled and whined to my teacher, Mr. Ehrlich, until he agreed to change my song. The show was in forty-eight hours and he had two conditions: first, I would be responsible for making the change to the nearly one thousand programs that had already been printed, and second, I would have to have the words memorized by the following day. I took the deal.

I spent the next day inserting slips of paper into programs and learning the lyrics to my new song. "After You've Gone" was catchy and easy to learn, and I was happy to be on the cusp of making my solo debut. The dress rehearsal went flawlessly.

On opening night, I was waiting backstage before my performance, admiring the singer before me and the bright lights of the set, when I turned to my friend Tonya, the stage manager.

"What's the name of my song?" I asked.

"After You've Gone," she replied, looking at me strangely.

"Right, of course," I said. I didn't wonder what it might mean that I couldn't think of the title of my song minutes before I performed.

I stepped onto the stage and was at once both blinded and dazzled by the lights. It was a full house, and everything about the night sparkled. This was my moment. And then I heard something that surprised me.

The accompanist was replaying the opening bars of my song. I'd missed my intro. I heard the measure replayed, opened my mouth and...nothing. Not a single word.

My mind completely blanked. The piano kept playing.

I began to move around the stage, in a sort of swaying dance, expecting any second I'd hear something familiar and the words would flood my memory, but I was wrong. The song played on, and I got nothing.

As the accompanist started the second verse, Mr. Ehrlich leaped to his feet. He was a table or two back, and I could see him mouthing something at me. The words perhaps? Advice to get off the stage and spare myself continued humiliation?

"I can't see you," I said, now rooted to one spot, still swaying, still humming.

The piano thumped on, through the second and third verse and I swayed. The spotlight fixed on me, as I performed not a single word of the song I'd campaigned so hard to sing.

When the music came to a blessed end, the audience hesitated. They were horrified for me, I can now understand, each thinking about what it must feel like to live every performer's nightmare. It took a minute for the applause to break out, staccato and stuttering, then quiet, like a small wave lapping the shore. I left the stage and went straight to the bathroom.

I was locked in a stall when my sister came in. Today, as adults, we are close, but not at that stage of our lives. During that era, we were sworn enemies. My bratty kid sister crawled under the stall door and patted my back as I sobbed. "I thought you looked very pretty," she said softly. When a person who regularly works to make your life a living hell tries to make you feel better, you know things are bad.

Want to hear a redemption story, that the second night was flawless, and I received a standing ovation? Nope. The second night I managed to remember the refrain once and broke out into a little dance number. It was a different style of disaster, but equal to opening night. The third night went no better. My humiliation was consistent and complete.

I stood on stage and forgot every word to a solo performance three nights in a row. A thousand people watched me hum, sway, and occasionally shout out a remembered word or two while improvising a spin, like an off-kilter ballerina struggling with Tourette's syndrome. It was a failure of epic, nightmarish proportions.

Think I am exaggerating the degree of this disaster? Perhaps you'd like me to follow my own advice and consider additional data to reframe this experience?

I offer the following additional data for your consideration: six years later, when I was back at my school to talk about the college I'd chosen, the vice principal passed me in the hall and began humming my song and swaying before moving on with a hearty chuckle. Two decades later, my choral director, Mr. Ehrlich, still tells this story when he explains why he won't allow song changes for *Dessert on Broadway* performers.

I failed—unequivocally, publicly, and repeatedly.

The *Dessert on Broadway* failure is one in a long list of failures I carry. The boom-and-bust first business. My marriage to my children's father. Conflict I didn't handle well with people I loved. The loss of more than a quarter of a million dollars in less than a year and the close brush with bankruptcy. The list of my spectacular failures goes on and on. And I'm grateful for the gifts present in each and every one of my disasters.

I realize that isn't how we normally look at failure. Perhaps you think I am unrealistically positive, viewing the world through rose-colored glasses. And you might be right. But looking at failure differently allows me to learn in ways I otherwise might miss.

Culturally, failure is tangled with shame and disappointment, among other negative emotions. But I've learned to think of failure like engineers do. When engineers design something and it doesn't work as intended, they recognize it as a failure and try again. There's no self-flagellation, shame, or giving up. There's only another attempt, informed by the first. In fact, engineers often welcome failure.

Dr. Henry Petroski, a professor at Duke University, is an American engineer who studies failure. He teaches both history and civil engineering and has written more than a dozen books. In the first, *To Engineer Is Human: The Role of Failure in Successful Design*, Petroski argues that failure is a necessary part of engineering design. He writes that lessons learned from failure can spark new understanding and technological advances.

Failure is feedback. Often painful, but feedback nonetheless. When we separate failure from negative emotion and shame, the information it offers is compelling. It presents us with unique gifts that, while available elsewhere, aren't quite as rich and as clear as when you're face down on the field or speechless in the spotlight.

Failure invites reflection. When we train hard for a race, practice daily, watch what we eat, and monitor our times and lose, we look carefully at our preparation. Maybe we could've switched our diet, shifted our practice course, added or ditched a layer of clothing. We carefully examine what worked and what didn't and improve our attempt the next time.

When we train hard and win, we assume that we won because we ate well or, worse, because we are good runners (see that fixed mindset?). We're the same athletes at the next starting line. Success doesn't inspire reflection or force growth.

Failure allows us to examine our expectations and assumptions. Why did I think I could win? What did I assume about my competition? Were those assessments grounded?

The reflection and examination of failure often prompt practice, innovation, and evolution. For me, the failure of my first dinner business caused me to carefully examine what I wanted, how I defined success as an entrepreneur, and, most importantly, what I was willing to do to get there. I reflected on what strengths had made me successful and what got in my way and contributed to my failure. While I remained passionate about helping busy families with a product that was simple and fairly priced, I didn't ever want to work in food service again. My successful second business still targeted the same population and focused on materially improving their circumstances but didn't involve perishable inventory, a physical location, or the need to be food-safety certified.

The founders of Instagram, Kevin Systrom and Mike Krieger, had no intention of shifting our culture to a place where no one eats before snapping a picture of her plate. They developed the wildly popular photo-sharing app only after examining the failure of their first idea, Burbn.

An app similar to Foursquare, Burbn (yes, named after bourbon) allowed people to plan meetups with friends, check in to locations, earn points, and share photos. But it struggled. Adoption rates were slow and features the team worked hard to build were underused. The app was too complicated, and Foursquare was already firmly established. It wasn't long before Burbn failed.

As Systrom and Krieger examined the failure, they were able to reframe that assessment. Burbn's users were sharing photos at a rapid rate; in fact, many only opened the app for that reason. They took that information (mined from the ashes of a fresh failure) and ran with it. They retooled the app to perfect the photo-sharing components.

Systrom and Krieger didn't get stuck grieving the loss of what they thought they could build. They didn't swirl in self-pity and shame. Instead, they took an objective look at what was happening and pivoted. Instagram grew to one million users two months post-launch and passed the billion-user mark in May 2019.

You met Bill Campbell, the coach to Silicon Valley in chapter 1. His work with Steve Jobs, Eric Schmidt, and Sheryl Sandberg powerfully influenced Apple, Google, and Facebook. His client list numbered in the hundreds, and most of Silicon Valley has benefited in some way from

Bill's wisdom; wisdom that was, in part, derived from the total failure of the first company he led.

Go Corporation was founded in 1987. The company intended to develop and sell portable computers, an operating system, and a digital pen and associated software. Go had an all-star roster of tech titans, $75 million in venture funding, and a solid product concept. In less than seven years, it failed completely; mired in lawsuits and facing stiff competition, Go shut its doors. No transfer of patents or proprietary systems, no spin-offs. It was well funded, appropriately staffed, and sold products that were the darlings of the tech world and destined to be commodities across the globe, yet it ended as a total failure. And for years, Bill used that failure as one of the most powerful leadership lessons of his life.

Failure was one of the things that propelled Bill Campbell to greatness and the critical change catalyst that transformed Burbn to Instagram.

Of course, we don't always fail, pivot, and succeed. Sometimes, we fail, fail again, and keep failing. That kind of failure, while painful and demoralizing, can grow perseverance and grit.

In 2012, the Center for Talent Innovation (CTI) surveyed more than four thousand college-educated professionals in companies like American Express, Deutsche Bank, Ernst & Young, Gap Inc., and Marie Claire to learn more about the components of executive presence. Presence is often talked about and seldom quantified, but studies show that it is a key characteristic of successful leaders. In fact, a quarter of what it takes to get promoted to the next level falls under the umbrella of presence.

When the CTI study broke down the components of observed leadership presence, gravitas emerged by far as the leading contributor to presence. The executives surveyed defined gravitas as showing grace under fire, acting decisively, speaking truth to power, showing empathy and emotional intelligence, and crafting and sharing a vision. One common factor emerges in developing these skills: grit. Grit and perseverance are the seeds of gravitas, and gravitas is the key characteristic of strong leaders.

Stewart Butterfield and Caterina Fake were not yet thirty in 2002 when they rounded up a handful of their favorite programmer friends and formed Ludicorp to develop and distribute *Game Neverending*, a multiplayer online game of massive, never-before-seen scale. The game was to be played in perpetuity—a person could play for all their life, unlocking locations and abilities as they progressed. It was a colossal programming challenge and an intriguing endeavor to the gaming industry. While Ludicorp secured significant initial funding, the magnitude of the challenge devoured it fast. By 2004, after writing an enormous amount of code, the team was struggling, needing more money to be able to continue development. To raise more capital, they had to prove progress. The team reviewed what they had that could be released as a stand-alone product and chose a photo-sharing capability embedded deep in the game. That is the inadvertent origin story of Flickr.

Yahoo bought Ludicorp in early 2005 for around $30 million. Butterfield and Fake continued to work on their game project as part of the new team. In the years that followed, the two married each other and divorced. They left Yahoo. The work continued. Butterfield carried on the multiplayer game dream after their separation and in 2009 formed Tiny Speck. The goal of Tiny Speck? To form a massively multiplayer online game, now named *Glitch*. *Glitch* raised $17.5 million and launched in 2011, but never attracted the projected audience. The online universe shut down in 2012.

In 2013, Tiny Speck released much of the *Glitch* programming under a Creative Commons license and launched a subset of the programming the company thought might have legs. That subset? Slack, the wildly popular messaging app.

Butterfield has now launched two massively successful

products. He's worth more than $1.5 billion and has been named the *Wall Street Journal* Tech Innovator of the Year and one of *Businessweek*'s Top 50 Leaders. Fake has seen similar success, serving as chairperson of the board for Etsy and being named one of the Fast 50 and *Time*'s 100 (along with Butterfield). Their current success is obvious and irrefutable. What is less obvious is that the road to that success was paved with failure, the loss of millions and millions of dollars in investor funding, a divorce, and repeatedly beginning again.

While they've still not launched a multiplayer never-ending game, the effort continues. Using the Creative Commons license, two follow-on versions of *Glitch* are in beta testing. That's grit in action, born of repeated failure.

Failure can create instant, powerful community. Tell a group of people your most embarrassing personal story. What you'll find isn't judgment and ridicule, but a chorus of "Me too" or "You think that's bad..." We can all relate to moments when things go awry, when we end up getting smacked in the face by the ball rather than dunking it. Revealing that vulnerable part of ourselves can bring us closer together.

These are the secret upsides of failure: reflection, iteration and innovation, grit, and community. These can be game-changing gifts—if we can access them. But when we are swirling in shame about a past failure or busy trying to avoid future failure, we miss these secret gifts. It's painful to stare failure in the face. But, if we can get curious about failure and work to understand it, these gifts can enrich and strengthen us.

These benefits only grow when we move from exploring individual failure to group or team failure. Groups or teams that face failure objectively and can block failure's shame-swirl reap powerful benefits.

The Post-it notes filling your fridge, bathroom mirror, and desk were born of failure. The story of how they got there is a great example of how companies benefit when they change their thinking about failure.

In 1968, Spencer Silver invented the adhesive on the back of today's sticky reminder. He was working for 3M at the time and looking to develop a strong adhesive for use in airplane construction. But he failed: the adhesive he created was pressure sensitive, light, reusable, and left no residue. It wouldn't work for airplanes, and it was quickly shelved.

In the years that followed, 3M repeatedly demonstrated its different perspective on failure. First, by actually shelving it. Sometimes, shelving is a euphemism for discarding, but 3M retained the formula. Silver adopted his mistake as a kind of pet project, spending five years circulating the formula inside the company and approaching product development teams. That's a second 3M difference: Silver didn't hide his failure; he made it quite public, sharing it with anyone and everyone who might be able to use it.

Engineers at 3M came up with lots of potential uses for the sticky stuff, even developing a prototype for a sticky bulletin board. Teams worked on ideas for years, finally in 1977 developing the Post-it note we know today. There's the third 3M difference: how many other companies would invest nine years exploring a mistake before developing a viable product?

Except the Post-it wasn't viable. Not yet. The limited release of Post-it notes in four cities flopped. They sold like woolen mittens in July. Almost no one bought them. Add another failure to the list.

Did 3M give up? No.

The following year, 3M sent Post-it notes as free samples with other orders. Nearly ten years after Silver invented the adhesive, 90 percent of customers receiving the free sample reordered the product. Post-it notes were finally born.

What would be possible if you shared your failures and

mistakes broadly? What if you could mine a reserve of ideas and products that were actually shelved to be considered later? Think of how you and your teams could innovate and create. Think of how nimbly you could address consumer and market need.

I recently spent a day with the executive leadership team of a newly formed media and technology company. The nearly dozen leaders had worked at what had been two strong competitors until this new company was formed. Most didn't know each other, and many were eyeing the others warily. Day one can be tough.

The founder and CEO of the acquiring company spoke first, sharing his story of forming the company with two friends in his basement. Then each of the rest of the members of the management team introduced themselves. Each had founded a company. Some started in garages, some in basements, some in their childhood bedrooms. Each leader sitting around that table had nurtured an idea, launched it into the public eye, secured funding, and built a team. Some of those companies had been forced to sell when the economy turned; some had shut down; some had spectacularly failed in other ways. None, except for the CEO and his friends' idea, had succeeded. They were all now sitting around a table working for someone else. And, on day one, sharing their stories of disappointment and failure.

That conversation surprised and delighted me as the coach working with them through the transition. Mergers and acquisitions can be sticky, filled with posturing that gets in the way of authenticity and connection. The frank way each had discussed his or her experience without shame or hubris delighted me because this openness held real possibilities for the team. The experience around the table, when mined for shelved ideas and gifts of failure, would hold the keys to the company's future success.

Fully embracing failure opens powerful possibility. When we divorce failure from shame and reframe it, we can capture the upside. Failure allows us to reflect, iterate, and innovate. Failure develops grit and community, for individuals and for teams. Grit and community drive innovation, creativity, and results at work.

My high school musical failure made me fearless. The worst possible thing that I could think of (as a self-involved teenager) had already happened to me. So why not reach higher or try harder? If I failed again, I was in familiar territory. My courage and confidence were forged in the fire of my disastrous experience.

In the next chapter, we'll talk about how to stand in the courage built by your experience—knowing how you got there and who you are without shame or fear.

KEY TAKEAWAYS:

- Reframing failure involves redefining it as an opportunity to learn, separate from shame.
- Failure allows for reflection, iteration, and innovation.
- Failure helps develop community and grit.
- Grit is the key ingredient for gravitas, the strongest driver of executive presence.
- Capturing the possibilities in failure benefits both individuals and teams.

REFLECTION:

- Consider a failure in your history with fresh eyes. What gifts did you receive from that experience?
- What do you notice about the link between failure and innovation in your work?
- How do you as a leader support learning from failure? What's working? What needs to change?

CHAPTER 9

How to Be Naked at Work (and Why It Matters)

"The moment that you feel that just possibly you are walking down the street naked...that's the moment you may be starting to get it right."

—NEIL GAIMAN

It's time to get naked.

Up until now, we've been in a pretty safe zone. We've introduced the lofty idea that there is no perfect path to leadership and there are no perfect leaders. We've talked about theoretical frameworks for how we process experiences and think about performance. We've been privately and cautiously exploring how we can better objectively evaluate where we are and what we've done, how we might reframe our negative stories, and how we can think in a radically different way about failure.

But the time for theory, exploration, and reflection is over. It's time to change how you show up at work.

None of this matters if you stop here. You may have a new perspective on yourself and your path up until now. You may be better able to evaluate your strengths and weaknesses. You may be writing and practicing new stories for yourself. That's all well and good. It may even be making you feel better, and that's terrific.

But those are not the reasons I'm writing this book, nor why you're reading it. This isn't a self-help book. **This is a leadership manual, designed with one goal in mind: to make you a grounded, confident, authentic leader who inspires teams.**

To do that, you need to be naked.

Being naked at work is a metaphor, of course. Please keep your clothes on.

Getting naked at work means dropping anything and everything you're doing for the sake of managing impressions, shame, pretense, and anything else that is not related to leading people powerfully forward.

Getting naked means trusting that you are good enough to lead. Your experiences up until now, including your mistakes and your failures, have prepared you exactly for this. Trust that you can access the full breadth of your learning to support your team. You can tap into the power of your failures to drive innovation and share your mistakes to foster connections.

Getting naked is about being human. It's about inviting others into their full selves by being your full self. The naked leader understands what she's good at and what she's still learning. She allows space for exploring failure, shame, and story. The naked leader is focused fully on the challenge ahead, not distracted by interference. She no longer invests time or energy into managing shame. The naked leader accepts herself fully and, in doing so, opens the door for the team to accept themselves and others fully.

Getting naked at work is leading from your truest, most authentic self.

Leading authentically and being human at work isn't for the sake of being liked or getting high scores on an employee survey. It is about developing high-performing teams and delivering powerful results.

It may feel like opening the door to humanity and vulnerability will muck up production at work. It may feel like it will take the team's eye off the ball and divert focus and attention from core, necessary deliverables. And I might agree with you if it weren't for one thing.

Humanity and vulnerability are already well established on your team and in your workplace. Each person at work carries the same heavy load of assessments, narratives, and failures that you do. That baggage is already affecting their ability to perform. You just haven't seen it up until now.

In 1999, cognitive psychologists Daniel Simons and Christopher Chabris designed an experiment to show how little we notice when we are focused on a task. The experiment, now famously known as the Invisible Gorilla, required participants to watch a video of people dressed in black or white shirts playing basketball. Simons and Chabris asked the participants to count the passes the players dressed in white shirts made.

About midway through the video, a person dressed in a gorilla suit walks to the middle of the screen, pounds its chest, and exits. Simons and Chabris surveyed viewers after the video ended and found that 50 percent of viewers never saw the gorilla. Half of the participants, people of all ages and backgrounds, didn't see a *gorilla* walk onto the basketball court. And they were sure they didn't see it.

Some argued that it wasn't there and had to be convinced by viewing the video again.

These results have been replicated many times in similar experiments in the years since. Videos have included other unexpected events, and the results hold. We see and respond to what we are paying attention to, not to what is actually happening in front of us.

If you, as leader, are not paying attention to the human, vulnerable qualities in your team, you won't see them. But that doesn't mean they aren't there. Not seeing or acknowledging those qualities simply means that you won't be aware of the full extent of interference you and the team are facing, and performance will suffer.

What does it mean to be an authentic leader? Merriam-Webster defines authentic this way:

> not false or imitation: REAL, ACTUAL (*an authentic cockney accent*), true to one's own personality, spirit, or character (*is sincere and authentic with no pretensions*)

Dr. Fred Walumbwa is one of the most influential leadership experts of the last two decades. In 2008, he worked with colleagues to define and study the components of authentic leadership worldwide. His work found four key characteristics:

1. *Self-Awareness*: Authentic leaders understand their strengths, weaknesses, and experiences. They know what is important to them and can articulate those values.

2. *Relational Transparency*: Honesty and clear communication are required to lead authentically. Leaders who play politics or violate trust aren't viewed as authentic.

3. *Balanced Processing*: Authentic leaders can see the full picture. Seeing the full picture entails asking for a variety of opinions, understanding all available data, and exploring possibilities.

4. *Internalized Moral Perspective*: Knowing and leading with what is ethically right and fair is a key part of authenticity.

At its core, authenticity is about knowing yourself, owning yourself, and acting in a way that aligns with your values and principles. An authentic leader shows up as her full self and devotes her attention to the team and task at hand rather than managing to external expectations. Authenticity is owning the truth about where you are, without interference from shame or hubris. Authenticity is connecting in a real, human way with other people at work.

Authentic leaders stand out because they live their truth while the rest of the world swirls around them. Authenticity and personal branding are phrases that have recently taken over the management and leadership sphere. There are thousands of books and articles on these topics, and entire companies who have capitalized on the trend by naming themselves some version of those phrases. You could spend the next full year, without sleep, listening to podcasts on authentic leadership. Authenticity is having a moment.

But does it work? Are authentic leaders actually more effective than their counterparts?

A 2015 study published by Dr. Biplab Datta in the International Journal of Leadership Studies unequivocally says yes. Dr. Datta surveyed more than three hundred professionals on their experience of authentic leadership, as defined by Dr. Walumbwa's 2008 study. Authenticity was measured by sixteen questions across the four components of authentic leadership: self-awareness, open relationships and communication, balanced processing, and internalized values and standards.

The study concluded that authentic leaders are better than their colleagues across the dimensions of both managerial and leadership effectiveness. Managerial effectiveness is about getting things done, leadership effectiveness is about enabling long-term strategy and inspiring others. From a managerial perspective, the authentic leaders studied in the experiment drove better performance on key business measures and overall goal attainment. Authentic leaders had fewer issues with negative attitudes and absenteeism and saw higher levels of employee satisfaction. When we consider leadership effectiveness, authentic leaders drove increased levels of respect and commitment from followers, and an enhanced team ability to solve problems and deal with change.

Remember Rose Marcario, the CEO of Patagonia? Under her leadership, Patagonia has implemented several policies directly tied to her personal values. One of the more well known is the parental leave policy. Patagonia offers sixteen weeks of paid maternity leave to mothers and twelve weeks of paid leave to fathers. It doesn't matter whether you're full or part time—if you work at Patagonia and have a baby, you're entitled to that benefit. When parents return to work, they have access to high-quality on-site childcare and nursing mother rooms that have soft furniture, locking doors, and a refrigerator to store breast milk. As a result, for the past several years, every single person who has left work to welcome a new child has returned. Every single one. The national average is about 65 percent. There's one example of the better performance, fewer absenteeism issues, and increased followership found in Datta's academic study.

Marcario firmly believes that supporting new parents

is the right thing to do, which aligns with Walumba's aforementioned characteristic of Internalized Moral Perspective: knowing and leading with what is ethically right and fair. She has worked tirelessly to convince other CEOs to follow her lead. She wrote a book sharing her philosophy and approach. She drafted and published the business case showing that Patagonia recoups 91 percent of the costs associated with her programs. And, most stunningly, she shares resources, time, and learnings with other companies implementing family-friendly policies at no cost. That's what authentic leadership and commitment look like in action.

Tucker Max and Zach Obront, co-founders of Scribe Media and its publishing division, Lioncrest Publishing, provide another example of transparent authentic leadership. Full disclosure: Lioncrest is the company that published this book. That's not a coincidence. As I was researching publishers for this book, Lioncrest stood out with its unique approach to business. Take this excerpt from the first page of my publishing contract:

> This agreement is intentionally written in plain English. We think the impenetrable lawyer-speak of modern contracts inhibits understanding, cooperation, and mutual benefit, which helps no one (except the lawyers). We want what's best for both of us, now and in the future, and we think plain English agreements help achieve that.

In short, the purpose of this agreement is simple:

You are hiring us, Scribe Media, LLC, to perform the services described below. This agreement is the official record of our relationship, and it lays out what we can both expect, who should do what and when, and what will happen if (god forbid) something goes wrong.

The full legal contract, including appendices, is only six pages long. It covers book creation and editing, distribution, and indemnity. It is double spaced and in twelve-point font. That transparent authenticity is why I chose to partner with Scribe Media. That authenticity drives results to their bottom line.

It's not only in the contract. Scribe Media works from a Scribe Culture Bible that outlines the values and principles of the group. The Culture Bible details how the team will interact, solve problems, and even fly in business or economy class on airplanes. The full document is public, which is interesting enough. What's nearly inconceivable is that the document is labeled as a working draft and is openly stored on Google Docs. Anyone anywhere can comment on it, and the team considers and responds to comments. That's transparency and authenticity at work.

Authenticity drives results. Whether it's funneling qualified candidates into your pipeline, driving revenue to your door, or keeping valued employees, leading authentically is universally more effective than the alternatives.

What the case studies and data don't show, though, is that leading authentically requires less energy than leading with a heavy load of doubt, shame, and other interference. When you are leading from the best and most true version of yourself, you are empowered and engaged. You are not focused on covering up, managing, or preventing shame. Your work becomes purpose driven—you lose the separation between work and life in the most balanced, healthy way. You are brought together as one full human at work.

I experienced that in my dinner-store business. Yes, it was a miserable failure financially; it included exhausting nights filling orders and long hours staring at financial projections. But despite that, it remains one of the most rewarding experiences of my professional career.

I was deeply connected to the purpose of that store. Helping working parents and putting a healthy dinner on the table for a fair price was important to me. I was passionate about that purpose and transparent about it with my team. For the first time in my life, I had no peers to compete with and no boss to perform for; there was no box to fit into, no single right way to do this work. I felt free. I was empowered by the four characteristics of authentic leadership.

My work in that business was the truest reflection of myself that I had lived until then. I hired a diverse team of energized, enthusiastic people and got to work. I brought my young sons into work and allowed others to do the same. I shared my philosophy of support for harried working parents, supplying both healthy dinners and a fun, social setting in which to prepare them. I welcomed ideas and feedback from the team and explored anything I thought might relate to our mission of helping busy families with dinner. In fewer than sixty days, the team was selling our product at a rate nearly double our initial projections. And it was fun.

Our energy was boundless. I loved being at work with the team, and the team loved our work together. The average employee turnover in the restaurant business is 75 percent annually; ours was next to nothing. When an employee had car trouble, she asked another for a ride to work. When someone was sick, another covered for her, and if the illness lingered, other employees donated sick days and dropped off soup. That team showed up for each other in and outside of work, and we are still at it. More than a decade after we worked together in any capacity, and after an ending where every employee was eventually laid off, we still have fond memories of our work and choose to spend time together.

My experience with authentic leadership is by no means

unique. Remember Kate, the chief HR officer succession candidate from chapter 6? She was struggling with what she thought she should have done rather than focusing on the problem at hand. Because of that, she was sometimes hesitant to fully express her ideas and opinions. The story she told herself was that it wasn't her place to question the actions of her boss or her peers when so much of what she did could have been done differently. So, she kept her observations to herself, stayed in her lane, and focused on getting her work done. When she did speak up, it was in a polite whisper. Her message was couched so deeply in corporate jargon and over-balanced by positive statements that people didn't understand it.

One of the pointed pieces of feedback Kate heard from her leaders as we started the coaching engagement was that she wasn't focused enough on leading her peers and speaking up to the C-suite. When she first heard that, she wasn't sure how it mattered. She was getting her work done, and her team was performing well. Leading her peers or trying to influence her superiors felt like extra work.

As Kate moved through her coaching engagement, she began to be more comfortable with who and where she was, and more accepting of her own unique perspective. She let her experience as she now understood it build her courage. She stopped focusing on the negative fallout that might happen if she spoke up and began to share her thoughts and ideas with her peers and manager. And people began to listen. She was building a powerful leadership brand.

Over time, her peers viewed her as a trusted ally, and her boss came to depend on her insight. Her colleagues reported that her executive presence had grown, and the board began to think of her as a versatile, capable senior leader rather than simply a very talented specialist.

And yet Kate didn't feel like this was extra work. By focusing not on managing what others thought of her (an impossible task to begin with), but on moving her team forward and sharing her wisdom, she began to feel more connected with the purpose and success of the full team. That, in turn, led to sharing her thoughts more often and engaging more authentically with the broader work of her company.

Kate grew to define her work as creating a workplace where talent could succeed and grow, and that purpose inspired her. Her full evolution of accepting herself, quieting her negative assessment and story, and bringing her authentic self forward made her feel better; she was less distracted, more positive, and energized. Her outcome? Kate gained the buy-in and support of the company's board and was formally named the succession candidate for the top human resources job in her firm.

Authentic leadership is not only in vogue; it also has powerful results for both the leader and team. The business case is irrefutable. But how do you move from leading as you are today to leading authentically?

First, start and end the day human. Notice when the interference of negative assessments or old stories blunts your focus and consider how often that happens to your team. Explore new ideas and options with common sense and curiosity. Notice when you're triggered by something and consider your emotions. Take care of yourself physically throughout the day, eating and drinking water, breaking when you need to. Encourage others to do the same. Your human experience matters and echoes the experience of your team, your colleagues, and your customers. Being aware of your own human experience develops empathy and emotional intelligence, two vital characteristics of great leaders.

Second, treat others with candor and compassion. The adage "Everyone is fighting a battle you can't see" is true. As you are human at work, so are your employees. Speaking to them candidly, without the interference of jargon, discomfort with difficult messages, or policy mumbo-jumbo allows them to hear the message clearly and own their response. As Brené Brown says, "Clear is kind. Unclear is unkind." Honoring others' experience and emotions with compassion will allow them to reduce their interference and distraction at work.

Before we move to the third step to implementing an authentic leadership approach, let's address some common interference my clients face when we begin this conversation.

The first objection most have is that there's no time to be human at work. I get it. I once functioned in back-to-back meetings too. I remember what it's like to be desperate for a bathroom break for hours, or to eat lunch on the run at three while late for the next meeting. I remember sitting in meetings as a call came through from the daycare and hoping desperately the baby wasn't so sick that I'd have to figure out how to go get him.

What I don't remember is what happened in those meetings. I was managing my interference rather than paying attention. And so are you and your employees. When you are leading an organization that functions without allowing time for reflection and rest, time away, or sick days, you invite all that interference in. It doesn't go away because you don't acknowledge it. **If you think you don't have time to be human at work, you don't understand all the time you and your team are already spending managing your collective humanity.**

The second objection I hear is that compassion and candor will really muck up the productivity of the team. You can't spend time holding everyone's bleeding heart in your hands. Someone must make the doughnuts after all. To that, I remind you that I'm not advocating you quit your day job to babysit the emotions of your team. I'm simply saying you are a more effective leader when you are aware of those feelings and their impact. You can respect someone's emotions and experience while also holding them accountable to standards. You can send a clear performance message compassionately. You can even fire someone with dignity and humanity.

HOW TO SHIFT TO AUTHENTIC LEADERSHIP

1. Be fully human at work.

2. Consistently treat others with candor and compassion.

3. Adopt and keep a beginner's mindset.

The third step in implementing your authentic self as a leader is to adopt a beginner's mindset, focusing on growth and progress rather than achievement. The beginner's mindset is the one that cheers when the baby takes the first step, rather than noticing the fall that immediately follows it. In the coming days and weeks, the beginner's mindset counts the steps no matter how many times the baby falls. And babies fall a lot. That same mindset applies here. You are a new authentic leader and you're going to fall often in the beginning. That's okay. As we learn new things, we make mistakes. In the next chapter, we'll cover some of the most common mistakes leaders make in the name of authenticity.

KEY TAKEAWAYS:

- **Getting naked and leading authentically at work has powerful results, for the leader and the team.**
- **Leading authentically requires self-awareness, transparency, openness to new perspectives and information, and actions that align with your values and principles.**
- **Teams with authentic leaders perform better.**
- **Authentic leaders are engaged with and energized by their work.**
- **To begin to lead authentically you must: (1) be human at work, (2) treat others with candor and compassion, and (3) adopt a beginner's mindset.**

REFLECTION:

- **When have you encountered an authentic leader? What was your experience of her?**
- **Thinking about your work in earlier chapters, what's still in the way of your authenticity?**

- When have you benefited from adopting a beginner's mindset?
- What might be possible for your team if you stepped boldly into your authentic self? What might be possible for you?

PRACTICE:

- Write the four markers of authentic leadership (self-awareness, transparency, openness, value alignment) across the top of a page. List your leadership characteristics that align with each marker. Where might you want to strengthen your approach?
- Write down your reasons for wanting to lead authentically and post the list somewhere you can see it daily.

CHAPTER 10

Getting It Right

"Success does not consist in never making mistakes but in never making the same one a second time."

—GEORGE BERNARD SHAW

Midday on August 18, 2018, Elon Musk tweeted, "Am considering taking Tesla private at $420. Funding secured." At the time, Musk served as both CEO and chairperson of the board of Tesla, and so was considered a reliable source on the company's plans. Both Twitter and the New York Stock Exchange (NYSE) reacted with enthusiasm, retweeting his message more than sixteen thousand times and pushing the price per share up 12 percent.

It wasn't the first time the frank and funny Musk had used Twitter to communicate directly with the public. Musk is well known for his tweets, often addressing rumors, company changes, and current events on the social platform. Many follow Musk for his humor, and indeed the August 18 tweet was a kind of joke. The $420 price per share he names is a slang reference to marijuana.

But the August 18 tweet also caught the attention of regulating agencies and investors who weren't laughing. The Securities and Exchange Commission (SEC) began an investigation lasting more than a month. In a settlement reached at the end of September, the SEC called Musk's tweet "false and misleading." Musk was forced to step down as chairperson for a period of three years, and he and Tesla paid a combined $40 million in fines. Musk paid more for using Twitter than Twitter has ever made.

Musk is unapologetically his authentic self, and his tweets are no exception. His comments to the public are often candid, incendiary, and sometimes outrageous. As one member of the Twitterverse put it, "The incredible thing about Elon Musk is you hear a tweet cost him $20 million and it's not immediately obvious which of his tweets it would be." Musk is the poster child for when authenticity in leadership goes wrong: his version of authenticity puts him in the spotlight and his company and employees at risk.

Authentic leadership is much more difficult in practice than in theory.

The path we've traveled to this point will broaden your perspective. You understand the positive impact your authentic leadership can have on your organization. You know how to objectively assess where you are and reframe stories. Those newly developed muscles will help you think flexibly about how you practice authenticity at work. A beginner's mindset will be important as you begin to shift your behavior, because as powerful and effective as it is, leading authentically can go wrong in many ways.

Years ago, I fractured my tailbone. It was painful and frustrating, and the doctor told me it would take weeks, even months, to heal. To minimize that time, I needed to stay off it. "Stand, don't sit" had to be my mantra. At the time, I was leading a large team in the small business division of a large national bank, and that meant lots of meetings, lots of sitting.

These were the days long before we understood sitting is the new smoking and stand-up desks became standard equipment in executive suites. Not sitting in meetings was going to be noticed, so I reluctantly added this item to my weekly discussion list with my boss. In our next one-on-one, I told her, with as little detail as possible, that I would be standing, moving, and calling in to some meetings for a time so I could heal.

She said she understood, and then continued to tell me, in

excruciating detail, about the time she broke her tailbone after a particularly amorous night with her husband. I heard all about what they were doing before, during, and after it broke. I heard about the ambulance ride and the months afterward when she (like me) couldn't sit. She then reminisced about what it was like to be young and active in that way and shared how much she missed her husband since he'd started drinking heavily. Twenty-five minutes later, I emerged from her office with the mental pictures she'd painted burned into my brain.

She didn't mean to traumatize me with her truth. She was, by any measure, honest and authentic in that conversation. She was trying to connect and make me more comfortable. But it went terribly wrong. She way overshared, and it wasn't for my benefit. Once she began the story, she dove into deep personal disclosure territory, centering the conversation around herself rather than tailoring it to help me.

Leaders inspire others to follow their direction and influence change best when they focus on others. Centering on others allows connection and learning. When a leader connects with others authentically and centers on her audience, she can learn more about their motivations, beliefs, and thoughts. That candid connection builds trust, a topic we cover in future chapters.

When you use authenticity to serve yourself rather than

your audience, sharing and authenticity can go wrong. No matter your initial motivation, sharing personal stories in an unbalanced or inappropriate way, with you in the spotlight, is authenticity gone wrong. My boss overshared, perhaps because she wanted acceptance, or perhaps because she sought confirmation of herself and her story. Regardless of her reasons, it created distance between us (lots of distance—I avoided small talk with her for months) rather than bringing us closer.

While that's a very clear example, this connection attempt often backfires more subtly. One of my clients had recently moved to a new team and was having trouble connecting with each of them on a personal level. To build relationships, he decided to share more of himself and began talking to them about his dog and his love of great wine. The intention and the topics are both appropriate, but his attempts fell flat.

Every day, he would walk up and down the aisles pausing to tell people about his morning walk with his dog or the last California vineyard he'd visited, but he never asked about others' dogs or if they liked wine. He didn't engage them at all. His team told me the morning update distracted them from their work and, in one direct report's words, made him look like "a pompous, tone-deaf ass."

My client centered interactions around himself rather

than authentically engaging his team in a balanced way. If the morning coffee talk had focused on team dog antics or included each team member's different but equally beloved hobby, he would have gotten the result he wanted.

Leading with authenticity also backfires when we use authenticity to excuse our behavior. "I'm a straight talker, take me or leave me," said a client of mine recently. "I'm too busy for small talk; when I'm here I like to get stuff done," said another. Those assessments, said privately to a coach, are harmless enough. What makes them troublesome in this context is that each statement was made in response to feedback from colleagues; in one case, it was about her brutal frankness and in the other it was about his seeming unwillingness to connect on anything but the task at hand.

"I am who I am" authenticity is usually about staying safe and comfortable. If we respond to feedback by asserting what we did was driven by our authenticity, we are defending our position, not receiving the message. We tell ourselves we are our best authentic selves; it's our environment causing the issues. **Hiding behind a fixed view of our identity means we don't have to change anything about ourselves. That feels safe, but it gives our circumstances more power than our choices.**

Some leaders believe authenticity requires taking emotional responsibility for others. Lisa, a managing director at a large professional agency, told me:

"I care deeply about my team. Supporting them in their development is a core value of mine. I know that Mike believes he deserves a raise. I told him that I'd be willing to fight for him. He's done excellent work. I'm worried we may not have it in the budget this year, and if he doesn't get a raise he'll be disappointed. He might even leave. What can I do to make sure I get ahead of this? I want him to understand that I'm fighting for him and I believe in him."

On the surface, that situation seems positive. A committed, authentic leader, Lisa supports her team. But she has moved from supporting to taking responsibility for an outcome she can't control. She's worried about Mike's reaction if he's not promoted and is trying to mitigate that.

The following week, Lisa learned Mike would not be getting a raise. She spent time and energy thinking about what he might say or do and how she might respond. That interfered with her own core responsibilities to lead and inspire her people and deliver on her goals.

Lisa and I spent an hour talking through the differences between authentically supporting and taking responsibility. Once Lisa grasped the idea that she could be supportive, develop Mike, *and* share the bad news about the raise without being responsible for his next steps, a big weight lifted. She shared the information, left space for his disappointment, and helped him consider what came next. That empowered Mike to make his decision (he stayed) and Lisa to stop investing emotional energy in taking responsibility for others.

Even when your authenticity centers on and supports others, doesn't function as an excuse for behavior you're not willing to examine or change, and keeps healthy boundaries, it can still go wrong.

I learned this the hard way. Early in my career as an executive coach, I was presenting to a group of senior colleagues. I wanted to show my best self and prepared carefully for the conversation. It started well, and my confidence and comfort grew as I moved through my presentation.

But then the web software I was using glitched, leaving my slides temporarily frozen. I tried in vain to restart the system and felt the pressure of seventy pairs of eyes and ears waiting for my next step.

I laughed nervously. "Please excuse me. I'm much prettier than I am smart," I said.

That was my authentic self. When I am nervous, I tend to

crack a self-deprecating joke, a feeble attempt to lessen tension or distract from difficult conversations. It's not a habit that serves me well, and it was particularly wrong in this situation, because it lessened my credibility with an audience I very much wanted to impress. It distracted from my content and created some interference for my peers.

It felt oddly sexist and wildly out of place. As a kind colleague told me later, it was very off-brand for me.

I'd suffered an authenticity misfire.

Authenticity has power, and it can work for or against you. Take, for example, a young man who wants to work in high-powered private equity funding in New York and has a face tattoo. The tattoo may well be a representation of his authentic self, but he almost certainly won't be hired.

Misfires and inappropriate applications of authenticity aren't always so obvious. I once was hired to work with a young powerhouse performer in exactly that kind of private equity firm. His boss was concerned about his appearance. No face tattoo, but his socks were too colorful, distracting from his executive presence.

As you decide how and when to show up as your full

authentic self, this is a core issue. Leaders must consider whether their demonstration of authenticity supports how others see their performance or distracts from it in their current environment. Are board members staring at your socks rather than your slides? Do they think your hair is too long or your skirt is too short?

This isn't fair. This isn't how it should work. But it is what it is. You may work to embrace your full authentic self, carefully evaluate when and how you show up as that self, and still come to realize that your current role isn't one that allows for your full authentic expression. Packaging still matters.

The 2012 CTI study that defined the components of leadership presence found that after gravitas, the next two key drivers of perceived presence were communication and appearance. Communication skills, both verbal and nonverbal, form 28 percent of our collective definition of presence, and appearance 15 percent.

Appearance and communication style are often rich opportunities for people to show their individuality. Geographic and cultural differences are woven all through our spoken language: when you were a kid, did you drink soda, pop, or Coke? What we wear, how we style our hair, and what we think is funny are all very personal choices.

Some of these authenticity markers showed up in the

study as executive presence detractors. Black employees who wear their hair natural, women who have long, brightly colored nails, and men who wear a hairpiece all may find their individual choices distract attention from their performance and reduce the perception of their leadership presence. So may people who speak too fast, show too much emotion, or use humor too often (this last one applies especially to women). **These are all deeply personal authentic choices. And they may work against you.** It isn't right or fair, but it is a very real issue for leaders to consider.

Elaine Welteroth is the former editor-in-chief of *Teen Vogue*, where she, in 2017, became the youngest person ever appointed editor-in-chief and infused the publication with social consciousness. In 2012, Welteroth had been the first African American ever to hold the post of beauty and health director at a Condé Nast publication. In discussing her groundbreaking work with the *Guardian*, Welteroth said, "When you occupy space in systems that weren't built for you, sometimes just being yourself is the radical act." Not right or fair, but true.

Your environment, role, and position in an organizational hierarchy may strongly influence when and how you choose to show your full authenticity. What might be costly for a junior employee—crying as you share your vulnerability about past mistakes, for example—might be groundbreaking for a senior leader. Purple and green hair might be celebrated as creative individual expression at a Silicon Valley tech startup and might be career-limiting on Wall Street. So how do you decide how and when to show up as your authentic self?

First, consider your environment. Is your workplace conservative or more progressive? What about your clients? Are you surrounded by expressions of authentic individuality or does the office look and feel more homogenous? How are people who stray from the norm received?

Second, consider your role and stakeholders. If you are a senior leader in your organization, expressing your authenticity can open the door to broad acceptance of others, both like and different from you. Below that level, you might consider the ramifications of expressing yourself genuinely. Does your company have others leading authentically, beacons you might follow? At what level? How are they like or different from you?

Third, consider your demographic. Are you a white man surrounded by other white men? There may be room for individuality. If you are a woman or a person of color in that same environment, the data suggests that there is less room for individuality. It's maddening and unfair, but if you are already "other," making yourself more so doesn't typically support ascent to leadership ranks.

Finally, if you choose to move forward, consider the missteps we've covered in this chapter. Think carefully about your motivation and your expression to ensure you're putting your best foot forward, no matter its sock.

Authenticity at work is a paradox. There are many reasons you want to be your full self at work, for your sake and the sake of your team. But you must carefully consider the ramifications of that choice for you in your current role. Once you've done the work to understand and accept yourself as a powerful leader, can you charge forward as that person without considering your surroundings? No, not always.

Consider the path Natalie chose. Natalie is an executive at a conservative bank. Her peers are mostly male, more tenured, and older than she is. Natalie is stepping into her authenticity carefully and not yet fully. She talks openly about her young daughter, and actively campaigns for family-friendly policies. She is a passionate advocate for work/life balance and speaks up when she sees issues that may negatively affect employees with family responsibilities.

Natalie is less comfortable pushing for diversity. Deeply troubled that only older white men surround her and that the company doesn't actively address this, Natalie believes the executive team suffers because they all think the same way. She believes diversifying the team with more women and people of color would improve performance.

But Natalie has heard, "You're one of us, Nat," more than once. She knows her teammates scoff at the idea of forced diversity, and driving the integration of employees who don't look like them will be difficult. She's not ready to tackle diversity now and may never be. As a single mom, she wants to be careful. She's chosen to start with pushing family-friendly initiatives and see where that takes her.

This is the approach that works for Natalie now. It's not fair or ideal, but it is her reality. Natalie can choose, when she's ready, to share more of her authentic self here or go to a workplace that aligns more closely with her values.

You will also face this personal choice. You will decide how much or how little of your authentic self to show. This part of your authenticity journey isn't about you being more or less than others at work but rather whether where you are is the right environment to appreciate your authentic leadership. If you don't feel safe being authentic in your organization, it may not be the right place for you. To paraphrase one of my favorite sayings: your authenticity may be too much for some people. Those are not your people.

I recommend starting like Natalie has, gradually and with a test-and-learn mindset. Be mindful of the common authenticity mistakes we've covered here. Don't center yourself or hide behind a shield of authenticity. Be careful about your boundaries. Begin to practice in a way that feels less risky. Understand how you're received, and then adjust as you see fit. Think about how you weigh the power and freedom of authenticity against potential consequences. This will be hard, and you'll learn as you go. We'll talk more about that in the next chapter.

KEY TAKEAWAYS:

- **Authenticity is powerful, but it can go wrong quickly.**
- **Regardless of motivation, be careful about centering on yourself rather than others.**
- **Don't use authenticity as a cover to ignore feedback or to support your comfort.**
- **Your authenticity should not blur boundaries into emotional responsibility.**
- **When considering whether you can be naked in your current work environment, think about your role, the culture of your team, and your stakeholders.**
- **If you're not sure or are feeling uncomfortable, start slowly.**

REFLECTION:

- What worries you most about showing up as your authentic self?
- When have you noticed authenticity misfires? What was at the source of each?
- When have you felt safest in your authenticity?

PRACTICE:

- Paint a worst-case scenario picture of how your authenticity might be received. Now consider what parts of that picture are likely and how you personally weigh the benefits and consequences of that choice.
- Make a list of beacons of authenticity in your organization. Where might you find inspiration or allies?

CHAPTER 11

It's Hard Because It's Hard

"A man thinks that by mouthing hard words he understands hard things."

—HERMAN MELVILLE

"This is way harder than I thought. It feels so messy and complicated. It's not even my job. I wish I could go back to what I was doing before."

I look at Tom, sitting across from me at his desk. His hair is ruffled because he's been running his hands through it, and his energy mirrors his hair. He looks and sounds unsettled, jumping from topic to topic and jiggling a knee.

Tom is the COO of a large construction company, and he's

learning to lead his team more authentically. He understands the power of candid, compassionate leadership, and he's fully bought in. He'd like to focus his employees' energy on the big-picture mission of the company and inspire them to follow him and the rest of the leadership team through a massive amount of upcoming change. He's worked through much of what we've talked about in this book, and he's been practicing showing up as his authentic self. And he's exhausted.

After a long pause, he says, "I really don't want to do this anymore."

Tom isn't alone. Every leader's journey to lead with compassion and courage comes to moments that are overwhelming, confusing, lonely, and hard.

We're conditioned to believe that when things are hard, we must be doing something wrong. Our internet feeds are filled with hacks to make everything from changing a toilet paper roll to peeling a banana easier. We read books about simplicity. We consume news in bite-size, easy-to-understand chunks. We receive and believe the message that hard is bad and easy is good.

Sometimes, things are hard simply because they're hard, even if we are doing them right. Take raising a teenager, birthing a baby, or training for a marathon.

Even when they are done exactly right, following every best practice and known method out there, they are hard, not easy.

That's what it is like to be naked at work.

When you lead with your authentic self, you strip off your protective armor. You expose your background, your thinking, and your mistakes. You don't have all the answers. You allow yourself to feel at work. You risk being judged for those things. You are vulnerable.

Leading transparently and authentically is lonely work. You're often in the minority. Many of your coworkers and perhaps even your leaders may still be focused on managing impressions or concealing shame and failure. That culture built the habits we've been unlearning together.

There is risk in showing up every day as your full self. Many leaders take cover in the certainty of a managed impression, not sharing transparently because it is safer than putting themselves out there. And it is, sometimes. Being the lone woman who speaks truth to power about a new, popular idea or being the gay man who lives openly in a conservative Southern Bible Belt culture doesn't feel safe. Being the only person in the room choosing vulnerability is difficult and sometimes has negative consequences.

You'll get this wrong, and that will make this feel even worse. You're a beginner. You'll share too much or for the wrong reasons. You'll take emotional responsibility for others, blurring the boundaries between you in the name of authenticity. I've experienced and seen this often.

When you make a mistake, it's easy to get discouraged. You might get pulled back into a negative story about yourself or your circumstance. You may begin to see yourself as the hero in retreat and, like Tom, begin to feel unsettled and uncomfortable.

Navigating the paradox of authenticity at work can be scary at first.

But, as Jack Canfield tells us, everything we want is on the other side of fear. You've worked hard to get to a place where you accept yourself and your path up until now. You have a clear sense of who you are and what you have to offer. Your candid, compassionate leadership will benefit your team. Keep moving forward. You can do hard things.

Adult learning theory emphasizes the power of productive discomfort, when we are uncomfortable but still able to learn. It involves moving out of your comfort zone enough to push the edges of what you know but not enough to be paralyzed with fear.

You likely felt productive discomfort learning to drive. You first focused on inserting and turning the key, learning the pedals, and adjusting the seat and mirrors. Once you'd mastered that, you carefully practiced in a large parking lot, a rural field, or a very quiet neighborhood street. You didn't navigate the on-ramp to the interstate that first day. If you had, you might never sit behind the wheel again.

When I work with clients, I encourage them to practice new behaviors. As we talk about where to start, we look for areas of productive discomfort, places to practice new things and be uncomfortable enough to pay attention but not be overwhelmed.

Those situations vary by person and work environment. Mark is a client who struggled with saying no. He's an affable guy who wants to please, a quality made infinitely more dangerous by his love for a shiny new idea. A dreamer and a pleaser, Mark never met a project he didn't greenlight. His team was drowning in the work he'd agreed to on their behalf. Resentment was building, and Mark realized he needed to learn how to say no.

Mark was so uncomfortable with looking someone in the eye and saying no that he couldn't imagine doing it at work. The very idea made his skin crawl. So, Mark began practicing saying no at home. He told his wife and family he was going to start practicing something new. Sometimes, when they made a request of him, he planned to respond with a simple "no." He started by setting up situations in which he could say no and be sure the person completely understood it was an artificial exercise. He asked his wife to ask him for a drink of water or to let the dogs out and in the same breath told her he was going to say no. Even then, when she obliged and made the request, the physical discomfort of saying no nearly doubled him over.

Mark started very small because his discomfort with the task was so big. He could never have said no to a peer at work without practicing first at home, because that would've been way outside his productive discomfort zone.

When I explained productive discomfort to a friend recently, he offered a metaphor that perfectly captured the concept.

"It sounds like math in school," Hal said. "Math gets harder every year, even for students who are good at it. Unlike reading, which you learn once and then apply, math is consistently challenging, *even when you're doing it right.*"

Exactly. **If you focus on productive discomfort, a hard task will remain hard even while you're improving.**

You start small and build. You may always be a little bit uncomfortable. It may always feel difficult and challenging. But you're making progress, and if you look back, you'll see how far you've come.

Tom and I talked through his frustration and discomfort. He was trying new behaviors in all situations and with each of his employees. He reflected constantly on what he was noticing, how that affected the story he was telling himself, and how he might reframe that story. He worked to lead authentically every waking hour. Of course, he was exhausted. He was well outside his productive discomfort zone.

I encouraged Tom to make a specific commitment to one or two behaviors for a short, defined time. He chose checking for understanding with his direct reports in one-on-one meetings for the next two weeks. Tom initially worried that focusing first on a small part of the work meant he wasn't all in. This goal felt too small to produce the change he wanted. When I explained productive discomfort, he felt better. Over the weeks that followed, Tom tried and mastered many new skills, each building on the ones that came before. The work remained difficult, but it wasn't overwhelming, and he could chart his progress.

This may be a short chapter, but it is the hardest part

of this work. Leading with courage and authenticity is a learned skill, and, like all learned skills, it takes practice. Practice can be tiring and overwhelming. You might get discouraged. Getting up and trying again when the authenticity horse bucks isn't easy. Even if you're getting better at it, it is still challenging.

Leading with courage and heart feels hard because it is hard. Do it anyway. This isn't only about you. When you do the hard work, it helps your whole team and organization. Authentic leadership has power that ripples far beyond you, and we'll explore that power in the next chapter.

KEY TAKEAWAYS:

- Being authentic at work feels hard because it is hard, not because you're doing it wrong.
- It's okay to feel overwhelmed and lonely, and to make mistakes.
- Like math, leading authentically in a way that supports your team may always feel hard.
- Find your productive discomfort zone and build from there, even if it feels small.
- This work will benefit you and your team in a way that far outweighs your initial discomfort.

REFLECTION:

- How might you feel when this gets hard? What can you do in anticipation of that feeling while still planning to persist through it?
- Where is your zone of productive discomfort?
- When else in your life have you carried out difficult tasks? What did you learn? How can that learning apply to this work?

PRACTICE:

- Write yourself a letter of encouragement to read when you need it.
- List the things you now do daily that were once hard.

CHAPTER 12

The Ripple Effect of Courage

"I alone cannot change the world, but I can cast a stone across the waters to create many ripples."

—MOTHER TERESA

It's brave to be naked at work. Showing up as your human, vulnerable self to lead is an act of unquestionable courage. That courage ripples through organizations, delivering value in unexpected ways. Your authentic leadership can become your organization's most valuable asset. Leading with courage, compassion, and candor can transform entire organizations and change lives. It can also deliver real dollars to the company's bottom line.

Teams benefit from authentic leadership. When a team

trusts that their leader is not concealing information, spinning a story, or diverting attention from a disaster, they are able to listen openly to the direction she provides. Teams who see the humanity in their leader are more likely to ask her questions, push for clarity, and escalate problems. These interactions speed the identification of roadblocks and ultimately solve problems faster than stifled silence. An authentic leader devotes her energy and efforts to solving the challenge at hand, enabling the team to do the same. She is not afraid to embrace failure and looks for and implements lessons learned without shame. Those lessons drive innovation and creativity. Clear communication, focused energy, and willingness to fail produces aligned teams able to find solutions to common challenges.

The differences between teams who trust their leader's authenticity and teams who don't drive results. **Teams that have authentic leaders perform better than those that do not.**

Gallwey's performance equation (Performance = Potential – Interference) explains this disparity. Teams who trust their leader is presenting authentically have far less interference than those who are working to understand what the unspoken message or true intent is in their leader's communications. Think of when you have worked for someone who you believe isn't being transparent with you. It likely felt unsettling and unsafe. Think of the energy you spent trying to understand how to best position yourself for success.

My client Josefina was hired as a senior director by a large hospitality company to build out their data security processes. She was specifically recruited because she had specialized knowledge the team lacked. Early in her tenure, Josefina noticed that her manager, Max, would often talk over her in meetings. He'd rephrase what she'd just said, address questions before she could, and take ownership for follow-up items he'd later delegate to her. When Josefina talked to Max about this, he at first denied it. Then he told her it was important to him that their colleagues and leaders viewed him as the expert. But Max wasn't the expert; Josefina was.

Since Max would write her performance review, Josefina was motivated to please him. She began to think about how she was positioning information and she included Max as she shared her ideas. She prepared him for difficult meetings, investing in teaching him privately before she taught the rest of the team. She began to view her role as both building out data security processes and educating Max enough for him to be viewed as a key contributor and expert.

That double duty had Josefina burning out fast. She estimated she was spending ten hours a week teaching Max, positioning him as an expert, or thinking about how she might do those things in the future. Twenty-five percent of a senior director's time was spent on managing the impression her boss created. If we estimate Josefina's compensation conservatively at $200,000 a year, she was investing $50,000 in making Max look good. Josefina was one of five people who reported directly to Max. If each of them faced the same challenge, Max's insecurities could cost the company a quarter of a million dollars in a single year.

This doesn't account for what investors would call the opportunity cost of that time. Imagine what the company could have achieved if Max had chosen to say, "I'm not the expert here, but I've brought in someone who is," and let Josefina's magic happen. What could each of those direct reports have done with 25 percent of their time focused on delivering the data solution the company needed? What could the company have done if they'd delivered their objective early, been able to capture data in a new way sooner, and used that data to deliver a differentiated customer experience or a new way to mitigate risk? Max's worry about how he might be seen by others cost that company, conservatively, well over a million dollars a year. The obvious irony? If Max had allowed Josefina and his other direct reports to do what each was hired to do, his results would have eliminated any need for worry. The company would have recognized and rewarded him for the team's strong results.

How many leaders like Max have you met? How much money have they cost your company? As we learned in earlier chapters, time and energy invested in creating impressions or managing shame doesn't have any return and their interference carries a measurable, significant cost.

Josefina didn't discuss the material cost of Max's behavior, though. Josefina simply didn't trust him. His obsession with being seen as an expert felt shallow and insecure, and his insistence on looking like something he wasn't unsettled her.

Mistrust is a prevalent problem in the workplace. Patrick Lencioni, a management consultant and prominent business author, identified the five dysfunctions of a team in his book by the same title, published in 2002. He named the absence of trust the most fundamental dysfunction. **Without trust, teams cannot perform.**

Merriam-Webster defines trust as "assured reliance on the character, ability, strength, or truth of someone."

Leadership experts Robert Galford and Anne Seibold Drapeau named three types of trust in the workplace.

The first is trust between employee and manager, which Galford and Seibold Drapeau call *personal trust*. Personal trust is the belief that a manager will do what she says she will, has her employees' best interests at heart, and can be relied upon to treat employees ethically and fairly. The second is *organizational trust*, the employees' belief that the organization has systems and processes that treat people appropriately, that communications will be prompt and transparent, and that a team will fulfill the promises it makes. The third is *strategic trust*, belief that the senior-most leaders in the company have the ability, vision, and resources to fulfill the company's purpose and drive success.

Authentic leadership is fundamental to each of these types of trust. Josefina couldn't personally trust Max to allow her to work without interference. She didn't trust the organization because the performance management system seemed to reward politicking and positioning over results, and her manager was able to actively block her impact. Strategically, Josefina had concerns about a company that would allow its managers to take credit for the work of their teams. Josefina's disappointment in her manager's lack of authenticity eroded her confidence in the whole company.

Conversely, when employees trust their managers, the team's potential for success grows significantly. Remember Harrison and Samantha, from chapter 2? Harrison was the CEO who had hired Samantha as COO to take over daily operations. He struggled with allowing her to lead because he wasn't sure what he would do once she took over.

Harrison and Samantha's relationship was ultimately successful and effective because they trusted each other. After working through their initial challenges, they decided to be fully transparent with each other and to trust the other implicitly unless given powerful evidence to the contrary. That agreement allowed Samantha to try new things, knowing she had Harrison's support even if she failed. Harrison trusted Samantha would raise any issues where she needed his help, and he stepped back. As their relationship grew, the trust increased. Samantha began to introduce concepts and processes from other industries. Harrison began to delegate more and more to his COO. Their mutual trust grew and eventually allowed Harrison to step away from the business completely and confidently. The business delivered financial returns they'd once thought unattainable. A committed, authentic connection can deliver those results.

Leadership authenticity and the trust it builds between people at work creates psychological safety, a cornerstone for high-performing teams. Harvard Business School professor Amy Edmonson has studied psychological safety since the 1990s and defines it as a "shared belief held by members of a team that the team is safe for interpersonal risk-taking." She elaborates: psychological safety is "a sense of confidence that the team will not embarrass, reject, or punish someone for speaking up."

If you are still investing time in shame, still focused on the possibility of your own embarrassment or rejection, you cannot lead a team effectively. If you don't feel comfortable with your story up until now, with your failures and missteps, you will not be able to create an environment where your team feels comfortable with theirs. **Group psychological safety is impossible without authentic leadership.**

In 2012, Google began studying teams in a two-year program named Project Aristotle. Google employees, psychologists, and sociologists looked at nearly two hundred teams. The findings were clear: teams with psychological safety built on trust of each other and their leaders, and carried out in their norms, far outperformed teams that were not psychologically safe.

Norms for creating psychological safety span a wide gamut. I've seen teams start a strategy-brainstorming session with a clear statement that no one will shut down any idea during the conversation. I've heard companies adopt and repeat phrases to convey safety; a senior leader at Capital One famously and consistently replied to news of failure or a glaring mistake with "There are no bad dogs here."

The best leaders understand the connection between psychological safety and innovation and make that clear to their teams. James Quincey, the CEO of Coca-Cola, tells his teams, "If we're not making mistakes, we're not trying hard enough." Criticized for the high-risk, seemingly low-reward, oddball acquisition of Whole Foods, Amazon's Jeff Bezos reminded his team and the watching world that his company's success and innovation is based on its willingness to take risks and be honest about the results. Jim Donald, CEO of Albertsons and former CEO of Starbucks, prints Monopoly's "Get Out of Jail Free" cards by the thousands to distribute to his teams. He sets the expectation that his leaders are to use them frequently. The message is clear: fail fast, often, and without penalty. Safe certainty pays lower dividends than big risk. These CEOs know if you want spectacular success, you need to be ready for spectacular failure too.

When we feel safe on a team, we don't invest time or energy in preparing for worst-case scenarios or defending ourselves from our teammates. We can focus on the challenge at hand. We can try improbable solutions and talk about when we are confused or don't understand something. We trust that the team is bound together by the challenge; we aren't ever working against each other.

When whole teams feel safe to fail, safe to bring up a wild idea, and safe to criticize an approach, the full organization benefits. Teams and individuals learn and share that learning. As we turn the volume up on diversity of thought and approach, innovation accelerates.

Consider when you've felt entirely safe on a team. Who was it that showed up to work on that team: your hero in victory or your hero in retreat? What did you dare to do on that team that you couldn't elsewhere?

Now consider what's possible if every person on your team—direct reports, matrixed partners, and peers—feels completely and entirely safe? What if they each devoted their full attention to the task at hand? What if there were no interference?

What could your team achieve? You have the power to create that environment.

The bravest team I've ever belonged to came together for one night, September 21, 2001. It was ten days after the terrorist attacks on the Pentagon and the Twin Towers, and the four major broadcasting networks were airing a hastily organized star-studded concert called America: A Tribute to Heroes, with artists including Faith Hill, Billy Joel, U2, Wyclef Jean, Alicia Keys, and Willie Nelson. Chris Rock, Robert DeNiro, Muhammad Ali, George Clooney, and Julia Roberts planned to speak. The concert was a telethon-style drive to raise money for the United Way's September 11 fund.

I was a call-center leader for Capital One, then a medium-sized credit card issuer. I handled inbound collections and led a large team of call-center representatives, each sitting in a small fabric-covered cubicle wearing a headset. Calls would come in throughout the day, and when my team answered each call, the customer account information would pop up on their screen. In a short, scripted conversation, associates worked with customers to bring their accounts current. A sophisticated routing system handled the call flow and distribution. A team of engineers constantly monitored its hardware brain, a complex machine housed in the center of our building.

On September 18, three days before the concert was to air, we learned that Capital One executives had volunteered our systems and teams to receive the pledge calls. This was long before internet payments went mainstream or donations happened via text. The phone call was still king. As people called the number on the screen during the telecast, the calls would be routed to our centers, and our employees would take pledges and answer questions.

While that sounds simple, the technical changes required to make that happen were enormously complicated. Operationally, the problem was equally difficult. We had no idea how many calls might come in, when, or from where. We didn't have a software system for taking pledges, nor did we have enough time to staff the call center appropriately. Without a script, how would our associates know what to say? How would they process payments? How would we monitor call volume and content?

Like many of my peers, I was eager to contribute after the horror of September 11. I wanted to do something to combat the powerlessness that gripped our nation. But this challenge seemed far too daunting.

My leader changed my mind. An Army Reserve helicopter pilot, Gene had lived through his share of impossible challenges. As he stood in front of us, sharing the long list of requirements to carry out this audacious task, he remained open and calm.

To the many questions we asked that he couldn't answer, he responded simply, "I don't know" or "I'll find out." He acknowledged that he also felt overwhelmed by all the moving parts of this project but was prepared to learn alongside us. He reframed our doubts and concerns by focusing our attention on what was possible and reminding us of the big-picture benefit of this activity. We would do this together.

I don't remember much about the days leading up to the telethon. I know we created lists of shift volunteers and walked through problem scenarios. I vaguely remember a staff all-nighter, with pizza boxes and two-liter soda bottles littering the conference tables as we studied call routing maps. I remember being nervous but not overwhelmed. When I think about the night of the concert, though, my memory becomes sharp, the focus clear.

The concert was simulcast on more than thirty-five network and cable outlets, as well as a dedicated website, America Online's homepage, and more than eight thousand radio stations. It was distributed to over 210 countries internationally.

We turned the phones on at nine that night, as the first performer took the stage. Many of us had already worked a full day getting ready for this moment. We were exhausted and nervous, not at all sure we knew what we were doing. And the stakes were high.

The calls hit like a tsunami. Within minutes, every warm body in the building was on the phone, some working more than one line at once. We had to abandon our careful plans for supervisor availability and scheduled breaks.

We hadn't anticipated the many calls from people who didn't speak English. To handle them, we fashioned a makeshift call transfer process, standing on desks with scrawled signs asking for volunteer translators. Many of us guessed the caller's language correctly, but sometimes we scrawled more than one sign. Spanish? Mandarin? French? Hindi? Hold times were long, and yet people didn't hang up. Callers cried, laughed, and gave the United Way their rent money and vacation savings.

The courage our leaders displayed as we prepared for that night was contagious. Their honesty and straightforward approach to the problem served as a powerful example. We weren't distracted by interference, wondering what might happen if we failed or jockeying to impress. We were safe to hit thousands of balls back over the net. We all had the same goal, and our unified focus drove powerful results. When the last call ended, our teams answering the phones had helped raise more than $200 million for victims of the 9/11 attacks.

I've been on powerful teams since, teams that have challenged the status quo, allowed and celebrated failure, and been led by authentic, transparent leaders. But that night and that team stand out in my memory as the clearest example of the ripple effect of courage.

When teams feel psychologically safe, trusting they are

united by a common goal, they can focus entirely on performance. They are not distracted by interference.

The team that put a man on the moon in 1969 had no time for interference. John F. Kennedy first proposed his idea on May 25, 1961, and met opposition from 58 percent of American people, according to a Gallup poll. Undeterred, on a warm September day in Texas in 1962, Kennedy told a crowd of nearly forty thousand gathered at Rice University, "We choose to go to the moon in this decade and do the other things, not because they are easy, but because they are hard; because that goal will serve to organize and measure the best of our energies and skills, because that challenge is one that we are willing to accept, one we are unwilling to postpone, and one we intend to win, and the others, too."

Kennedy believed in his purpose. Many others did not. His detractors thought his vision was far too expensive, could jeopardize the future of our military, or was "just nuts." NASA's program lagged woefully behind that of the Russians, and the cost was staggering. Space program physicists wanted more time.

But if the space team didn't have more time, they did have the resources to build a unified, focused effort. They worked on rapid development and exploration, and discarded ideas quickly. As shown in the 2016 historical film *Hidden Figures*, the demand to innovate allowed for expanded roles for women and people of color on the team. That willingness to work together differently combined with a broader base of experience led to faster innovation. The team had a bold agenda and made big bets to achieve it. NASA beat Kennedy's deadline by nearly five months.

Teams united behind an authentic leader and a common purpose can become self-sustaining and high-performing. People willingly devote extra time and energy to the cause. I once answered a call from a colleague late on a Saturday night. "I've thought about how we can solve the problem we were talking about Thursday," he said. "Hear me out..." We spent nearly an hour on the phone, and I arrived early to work on Monday, eager to put his idea into practice. That's what it was like being on a team with my leader at the time, a gregarious, quick-witted dreamer who'd rallied us authentically to his cause. We had plenty of enthusiasm for the task at hand because we believed in him.

We see the ripple effects of courage every day in our culture. Oprah Winfrey changed the face of talk-show television by bringing her true and full story to the table. Her audience learned about her history of sexual abuse, her journey to self-acceptance, and her focus on continuous learning. In repeating the vulnerable mantra of her good friend Maya Angelou, Oprah taught generations of viewers to "know better, do better." Her focus on authenticity forged such a strong connection with strangers that she's built a media empire to continue to share her message with her devoted fans.

Your authentic leadership can be the catalyst that delivers measurable, material value to your organization. Your personal transformation will clear the path for your team's own courage and drive results. Each productive gain you make in your own performance by redirecting energy from shame or spin to bringing your best to the challenge at hand, your team will echo and multiply. Each of the current and future leaders who work for you will learn from your example what it means to lead authentically and the power of dropping the armor so many wear at work. The ripple effect of your courage will transform your organization.

KEY TAKEAWAYS:

- Teams with authentic leaders perform better than others.
- Authentic leadership reduces interference, delivers material value, builds trust, and creates psychological safety.
- Lack of authentic leadership costs companies time and money and robs organizations of potential.

- Authentic leaders build all three kinds of trust: personal, organizational, and strategic.
- Trust creates a psychologically safe environment for your team.
- Safe teams with authentic leaders don't face issues with engagement, political jockeying, or groupthink. They innovate fast and drive results.
- Your courage acts as a beacon for your team, and its effects will ripple and grow through your organization.

REFLECTION:

- What types of trust fractures do you see at work? How might your authenticity help heal that trust?
- How does it feel to be psychologically safe? What are key markers for you that you are safe?
- When have you felt the ripple effect of a leader's courage?
- What fears remain about leading authentically? How do you feel about those when you think about the potential benefit to your team?
- What is your brave vision for your team?

PRACTICE:

- Lead your team in a conversation to define a new norm for the group that is focused on developing psychological safety.
- Talk with a supportive peer about your vision and plan to lead authentically. Share your purpose and ask what benefits they believe your team will experience.
- Write a one-page description of the safe team you will lead.
- Set a timeline for your transformation at work.

Conclusion

"Welcome to my homecoming
Yeah it's been a long time coming
Lot of fights, lot of scars, lot of bottles
Lot of cars, lot of ups, lot of downs
Made it back, and here I stand, a better man."

—DIDDY, "COMING HOME"

"The last year has changed my life," Michael said. "I mean it; everything has changed." He is red in the face, gripping my elbow and leaning toward me with an urgency I've seen in him before. His eyes are glistening. It's an odd picture to anyone watching us at the downtown members-only club where we've met for lunch. Michael is a big, imposing figure, and if you didn't hear us talking, you might misinterpret his intensity as anger. But he's not angry. Not anymore.

When Michael and I met, he was deeply and powerfully angry. It wasn't obvious in the beginning. During our first meeting, I found him to be charming and personable. He joked easily and spoke openly about his role leading operations at the national media company where he works. It was when I interviewed his team that I learned about his temper. His team found him charming and personable, too, but saw a dark side more often. Michael struggled with conflict, punished employees who disagreed with him, and didn't accept feedback. He was a powerful motivator of his team when he was at his best; at his worst, he destroyed relationships and burned bridges.

Michael wasn't surprised by his team's feedback. He knew about his temper. He'd lived with it, at home and at work, for years. What he didn't know was what caused it or how to control it. It seemed to flash out of nowhere and burn white hot. As we began our six-month engagement, we started peeling back the layers of that challenge. We looked for what stood in the way of him controlling his emotions. What made him lash out even when he knew better?

Michael grew up poor and started working as soon as he turned fourteen. He changed oil, hauled hay, and worked on construction crews to help his family and earn enough money for a car. He eventually put himself through school, working during the day and studying at night. It took him six years, and his first job out of college was managing the same oil change shop where he got his first job.

Michael was a good worker and a charismatic guy. His shop sold more oil changes than any other in town, and he caught the attention of a local car dealer. That man mentored him, teaching him the ropes of a bigger business. Despite his humble beginnings, Michael bootstrapped his way up a corporate ladder of his own making.

As we explored his story, Michael began to think he was angry at his team for not recognizing that he was really one of them. He thought they saw him as a corporate cog, not as he saw himself: the common man who'd caught a break or two and ended up in leadership.

That explained his anger, but it wasn't the answer. As we talked more, Michael realized that underneath the anger was a feeling of worry and shame. He didn't feel like he'd earned the right to lead this team. He'd barely made it through college. He'd gotten his jobs through a series of lucky breaks. What if the team found out and thought he didn't know what he was doing? What if he really didn't know what he was doing? What if they realized he was just scraping by, overwhelmed by the work and the pressure, and feeling like a dinghy tossing in a turbulent sea?

His quick anger when pushed or questioned wasn't

offense; it was defense. Michael didn't believe he was fit to lead. He thought it was only a matter of time before others saw through his façade. Michael was collapsing under the weight of that future potential shame.

Michael and I spent weeks reframing his blue-collar experience to allow him to see how it served him in this role. He let go of his idea of the leader he should be, the background he should have. He began to understand his experience could be a connection point with his team, many of whom shared his story of humble, rural beginnings. I encouraged him to stop defending and isolating himself and to begin partnering more authentically. He came to realize that what he'd done up until now mattered less than what he could do moving forward. He focused his attention on what the team needed from him to achieve their goals, rather than what he needed from them to feel safe. He started asking curious questions, showing his vulnerability, and sharing credit with colleagues. He made mistakes and it was incredibly difficult. He kept at it.

Michael started practicing the same new skills at home. Instead of making all the financial decisions and taking full control of the future planning for the household—as he'd once believed he should—he began to talk openly with his wife about what he wanted and explored how that overlapped with what she wanted. He did the same with his adult son.

Michael and I worked together on this process for six months, and he continued the work on his own for the rest of the year. That brought us to this day, our one-year check-in.

Michael shared with me that his team had outperformed their goals by a significant margin. He'd been offered an expanded role. His team had elevated ideas to improve their processes and individual team members had stepped up to lead those initiatives. He and his wife were closer than ever. "I feel like I'm married to a different person," he told me, "but I'm the one who changed."

By reframing his story to drop shame, Michael called forth his hero in victory. He stepped into his full authentic self, as vulnerable and difficult as that was, and was now reaping the benefit.

"I didn't think this could ever happen," he told me.

Michael may not have thought this transformation was possible, but I always knew it was.

My work with hundreds of leaders has proven, repeatedly, that we have the power to transform ourselves and our teams. It doesn't take years of therapy or expensive degree programs. It takes awareness, intention, effort, and a path. You have the power to reframe your story to eliminate shame and call forth courage. Living in that authenticity will change you and your team for the better.

I wrote this book to show leaders how to be fearlessly authentic at work, and to make the case for how that authenticity will transform your team and your organization. Who you are, exactly as you are, is enough. You are the right leader for your team at this exact moment. When you can quiet the noise in your head to allow your truest, best self to come forward, you will have everything you need to powerfully lead your organization into the future.

It begins by understanding that there is no perfect leader prototype. All leaders have the capacity to deeply and powerfully impact teams, no matter their approach or background. We see it with college dropouts who form tech companies worth billions. We see it with women juggling families and minimum-wage jobs who start multimillion-dollar operations at the kitchen table during the baby's nap time. We see leaders who are introverts, extroverts, taskmasters, or visionaries. All kinds of leaders can be effective.

Reaching your peak performance is often about removing obstacles. And while some obstacles are obvious, like funding shortages, geographic distance, or lack of concrete knowledge, most of the obstacles for leaders exist within themselves. You might be able to name your obstacle: Did you screw something up early on and decide you're not cut out for this? Do the gremlins whisper, in the familiar voice of your father, that you've always been a follower or have wild, unrealistic ideas? Did you once hear your mother call you a spectacular failure? Those are stories you tell yourself, based on your personal view of your experience in the moment, and they have the power to limit or serve you. Your narrative isn't objectively true; it is the story you've crafted and chosen to believe over time. Your story is within your control; you can change it to serve you.

You might not know your obstacle yet. You might know it's there only by what it is preventing you from achieving—like knowing a rock is under the water by watching how the current swirls and flows around it. My bet, though, is that it is some form of shame. Shame whispers that you are not enough, not now or in the future.

Shame sucks up time and resources. It is an investment of energy and attention that you will never get back. Worrying about what's already happened is useless, as is fearing a future you can't control. Remember, You Are Here on the map, regardless of how you got here. As one of my more colorful clients said, "Covering your ass just makes it look like that's where your head is."

Focus instead on where you are. What have you achieved?

What have you learned? Explore your story up until now. Make a grounded assessment of your strengths and weaknesses.

If parts of your story are painful, look closer. How might you reframe those experiences to better serve you? Remember, this isn't about an objective truth—that rarely exists. This is about understanding how you view yourself and how that shapes your performance. Does it help or hurt you?

Even full and abject failure can be reframed, if not in the sequence of events then in the outcomes. Mine your failures for gifts. Failing allows for reflection, iteration, and innovation, and develops community and grit. Remember, many leading companies now actively embrace failure as a necessary stop on the road to success. Fail, get up, and move on.

Once you've understood who you are and explored what your unique perspective and contribution is, bring that full-strength authenticity to work. Connect humanly, and be transparent and honest.

But do it smart. There's a reason Adam Grant, the author and Wharton psychology professor, published an opinion piece in the *New York Times* arguing, "unless you're Oprah, 'be yourself' is terrible advice." Authenticity, if it is centered on you, can backfire. Set your intention to be authentic in service to others, whether that be by fostering human connections, sharing your learning, or being vulnerable and open to the contributions of others. Even when your intentions are good, your authenticity can misfire. This isn't easy.

I was asked recently, "What happens once a leader masters authenticity?" I had to answer with my experienced truth, which is: I'm not sure we ever really master leadership authenticity. Gremlins whisper to everyone. People make mistakes. Companies don't always reward the authentic behaviors. Peers and supporters often advocate for safety over authenticity.

You may have noticed that I chose the female pronoun to refer to generic leaders throughout this text. I made that deliberate choice to contribute to shifting the entrenched, unconscious perception of leaders as male. It wasn't my original idea: Ben Horowitz, the CEO, author, and father of daughters made this same choice in his book *The Hard Thing about Hard Things*. My editor asked me to review this choice, suggesting that perhaps readers would believe this book was exclusively for women (it isn't). It might be safer to use a gender-neutral pronoun, she wrote.

Her feedback made me second-guess my choice: would I alienate readers by choosing a female pronoun? My confidence faltered, and I considered shifting to the more generic "they." I ultimately decided to move forward in the way that is most authentic to me: I believe all people can be good leaders and I also believe women are vastly underrepresented in leadership texts. Even now, with years of experience behind me, I heard the gremlins whisper and carefully considered the ramifications of my authentic choice.

Showing up as your full self is hard, never effortless. It is a deliberate, practiced act of courage.

But that deliberate act, as difficult as it is, pays incredible dividends. Authentic leaders build psychological safety, and that psychological safety makes magic happen. Teams innovate, create, and perform at levels even they might have previously thought unattainable. And that courage in leadership ripples through teams and organizations, driving exponential gains in performance.

I don't share this with you as a theoretical exercise. I have seen this played out in black and white on the pages of the *Harvard Business Review*, *Forbes*, and *Fast Company*. I've walked this path with clients in the C-suite of the companies I support. And I have also lived it.

I have looked in the mirror and thought, "Who am I to do this?" I have scanned a room and felt certain I was the least qualified leader present. I have told myself the story that I am less than, not enough, and faking my way through it so frequently that I knew it by heart and almost believed it was true.

And I have done the hard work I'm telling you about. I've checked my facts versus my assessments. I have wrestled to reframe my stories. I have mined my spectacular failures for learning, even when reliving those moments has been so painful that years later tears sting my eyes.

And I have been transformed. I have brought the full weight of this work forward in service to others, and I have watched it change the course of leaders' lives and the paths of the companies they serve.

You are exactly the right leader for your team, right now. Each experience, misstep, and unique characteristic can fuel your performance. And when you believe that, your world and work will transform.

Do this work. Keep at it when it is hard and watch what happens. And then, please, tell me all about it. I'm collecting stories for future publication and would love to hear about your experience. Please email me directly at Danessa@avenue8advisors.com and tell me about your journey.

Until then, be brave. Get naked at work. Show us who you really are and capture what's possible. The world is waiting for your hero.

Acknowledgments

I have been gifted a rich and varied set of experiences and people in my life. Each has shaped my path and contributed in some way to this book. I'd be lying if I said each of the experiences was magical in the moment—as you already know, many were painful and some humiliating. But the truth of it is, I've always been lifted and strengthened by the people surrounding me. And I am ever grateful.

First, I'd like to thank those who take up the mantle of leadership and strive do it well. It isn't easy. It requires vulnerability and humility. Those that honor and work at this skill are beacons for all of us. Thank you especially to the many strong leaders I've had in my career; I saw and remember you.

Second, I'd like to thank my clients. Many of you might think you recognize yourselves in this text. Rest assured, you don't. So many of the stories we think are painfully and privately unique are actually shared with others. In trusting me with your unvarnished experience, your aspirations, failures, missteps, and successes, you have allowed me to see the universal nature of a leader's journey. I am grateful to you for trusting me to accompany you on yours. Thank you. This "job" has been one of the greatest privileges of my life.

I would not have this job without the world-class team at the Georgetown University Institute for Transformational Leadership. Each instructor and staff member brought their full authentic self forward in service to my cohort of coaches (go 49-ers!) and we are richer for it. I want to especially thank Mike McGinley, who, upon meeting for coffee on a cold winter morning and listening to me consider my next step, looked me dead in the eye and said, "You must go to Georgetown." Mike, you were right. Thank you.

To the team at Scribe Media, thank you for helping me bring this book to life. Tucker, Hal, and Emily: I trusted you from the start, and again and again you showed yourselves to be worthy of that trust and more. Your feedback and support made this book clearer, crisper, and much more interesting. To my editor, Nicole, thank you for painstakingly answering my questions in the margins and being brave enough to take a different position in service to my finding and holding my own. To my publishing team, thank you for bringing this message to life.

To my colleagues in the coaching space, thank you for your generosity as I've navigated this process. I'm grateful to have so many worthy peers. Kathy Gallo and Jonathan Kirschner, especially, thank you for your steadfast support and inspiring example.

I'd like to thank my friends, who see the unedited authentic version of me at every turn. You have listened to me work through the lessons I've captured here over dinner, on long walks around the lake, and in endless text chains. Ann, Kathleen, Michelle, Michele, I am especially grateful for the love you've given me. Jay, I'm grateful, always, for the frank talk and inspiration. My notes from the conversation that started this book are still in my top drawer. Thank you.

I was raised by two people who taught me to believe all things are possible. My mother has always been a creative, inspiring, loving force in my life, and it is because of her that I dare spectacularly. My father has steadfastly supported me at every turn, helping me negotiate my very first salary, putting together sneeze guards at my first business, and painstakingly editing this book. My sister, brother, and brother-in-law have always inspired me with their courage, innovation, and creativity. I'm so grateful to have the love and support of my family and to meet them every Tuesday for tacos. Thank you. I love you all.

To Sebastian, Colin, and Ellison, the greatest joy I know is being your mom. I love you like crazycakes. Lauren, Mallory, and Hunt, I'm so glad you're in my life and love you too. Remember that being brave isn't acting without fear. Being brave is listening to your own voice, considering how that voice can serve the world, and acting in spite of the fear you feel. May you all dare spectacularly, loves.

And finally, to my beloved JB, you told me stories about myself I'd forgotten. Thank you for helping me remember who I am and loving all of me. You inspire my courage, capture my heart, and make me a better person every day. Thank you for your steadfast, enthusiastic support (and tireless comma editing). I love you, Darlin'.

References

Bradley, Ryan. "The Woman Driving Patagonia to Be (Even More) Radical." Fortune. September 14, 2015. https://fortune.com/2015/09/14/rose-marcario-patagonia/.

Brown, Brené. Brené Brown: Shame v. Guilt. January 14, 2013. https://brenebrown.com/blog/2013/01/14/shame-v-guilt/.

Datta, Biplab. "Assessing the Effectiveness of Authentic Leadership." International Journal of Leadership Studies 9, no. 1 (2015): 62–75.

Doyle, Glennon. Instagram. March 2019. https://www.instagram.com/glennondoyle/p/Bvg3fxgBh6d/.

Duhigg, Charles. "What Google Learned from Its Quest to Build the Perfect Team." New York Times Magazine, February 28, 2016.

Flood, Allison. "JK Rowling Says She Received 'Loads' of Rejections Before Harry Potter Success." Guardian, March 24, 2015. https://www.theguardian.com/books/2015/mar/24/jk-rowling-tells-fans-twitter-loads-rejections-before-harry-potter-success.

Galford, Robert, and Anne Siebold Drapeau. "Enemies of Trust." Harvard Business Review, February 2003.

Garber, Megan. "Instagram Was First Called 'Burbn'." Atlantic, July 2, 2014. https://www.theatlantic.com/technology/archive/2014/07/instagram-used-to-be-called-brbn/373815/.

Goldman, Jason. "Why Bronze Medalists Are Happier than Silver Winners." Scientific American, August 9, 2012. https://blogs.scientificamerican.com/thoughtful-animal/why-bronze-medalists-are-happier-than-silver-winners/.

Grant, Adam. "Unless You're Oprah, Be Yourself Is Terrible Advice." New York Times, June 5, 2016.

Hewlett, Sylvia Ann, Lauren Leader-Chivée, Laura Sherbin, Joanne Gordon, and Fabiola Dieudonne. Executive Presence. New York: Center for Talent Innovation, 2012.

Horowitz, Ben. The Hard Thing about Hard Things: Building a Business When There Are No Easy Answers. New York: Harper Business, 2014.

Ibarra, Hermania. "The Authenticity Paradox." Harvard Business Review, January–February 2015.

Kiss, Jemima. "Google CEO Sundar Pichai: 'I don't know whether humans want change that fast'." Guardian, October 7, 2017. https://www.theguardian.com/technology/2017/oct/07/google-boss-sundar-pichai-tax-gender-equality-data-protection-jemima-kiss.

Lencioni, Patrick. The Five Dysfunctions of a Team. San Francisco: Jossey-Bass, 2002.

Lipton, Bruce. The Biology of Belief: Unleashing the Power of Consciousness, Matter & Miracles. Hay House, 2006.

Lumb, David. "This Story about Slack's Founder Says Everything You Need to Know about Him." Fast Company, February 12, 2014. https://www.fastcompany.com/3026418/this-story-about-slacks-founder-says-everything-you-need-to-know-about-him.

Magnotta, Andrew. 2018. "Dave Mustaine Says Lars Ulrich Is Scared of Performing Alongside Megadeth." I Heart Radio, June 11: https://www.iheart.com/content/2018-06-11-dave-mustaine-says-lars-ulrich-is-scared-of-performing-alongside-megadeth/.

Markman, Art. "It worked for Google's CEO: This is the best way to respond to a tricky interview question." CNBC. June 20, 2019. https://www.cnbc.com/2019/06/20/it-worked-for-google-ceo-sundar-pichai-how-to-answer-a-tricky-interview-question.html.

McAndrew, Siobhan. "Patagonia CEO: Open childcare center to get more women in top posts." Reno Gazette Journal, June 1, 2017. https://www.rgj.com/story/news/education/2017/06/01/patagonia-ceo-open-childcare-center-get-more-women-top-posts/363761001/.

Melfi, Theodore, dir. Hidden Figures. 2016.

Merriam-Webster. Accessed 2019. https://www.merriam-webster.com/.

O'Callaghan, Jonathan. "A Single Tweet Just Costs Elon Musk $20 Million and Twitter Is Having a Field Day." IFL Science. October 1, 2018. https://www.iflscience.com/technology/this-tweet-just-cost-elon-musk-20-million-and-twitter-is-having-a-field-day/.

Official Pete Best. Pete Best. 2018. www.petebest.com.

Patinkin, Jenny. Instagram. March 27, 2019. https://www.instagram.com/p/BvgrE2hFovg/.

Ronson, Jon. "Monica Lewinsky: The Shame Sticks to You Like Tar." Guardian, April 16, 2016. https://www.theguardian.com/technology/2016/apr/16/monica-lewinsky-shame-sticks-like-tar-jon-ronson.

Sandberg, Sheryl, and Adam Grant. Option B: Facing Adversity, Building Resilience, and Finding Joy. New York: Knopf, 2017.

Schmidt, Eric, Jonathan Rosenberg, and Alan Eagle. Trillion Dollar Coach: The Leadership Playbook of Silicon Valley's Bill Campbell. New York: HarperBusiness, 2019.

Simons, Daniel, and Christopher Chabris. The Invisible Gorilla: How Our Intuitions Deceive Us. New York: Harmony, 2011.

Vedantam, Shankar. "Clicker Training for Dogs Is Adapted to Help Surgeons Learn Quickly." NPR Morning Edition. June 12, 2018. https://www.npr.org/2018/06/12/619109741/clicker-training-for-dogs-is-adapted-to-help-surgeons-learn-quickly.

Walumbwa, Fred, Bruce Avolio, William Gardner, Tara Wernsing, and Suzanne Peterson. "Authentic Leadership: Development and Validation of a Theory-Based Measure." Digital Commons@University of Nebraska at Lincoln, February 2008.

About the Author

DANESSA KNAUPP is an executive coach, leadership expert, and keynote speaker. Danessa spent more than twenty years as a CEO, entrepreneur, and Fortune 100 executive before completing Georgetown University's executive coaching program. Today, she blends that first-hand experience and education with the shared wisdom of her hundreds of executive clients to show leaders how to lead powerful teams with courage, candor, and compassion. Her clients lead multimillion-dollar companies across industries and regularly credit their success to the Naked at Work process. Danessa lives in Virginia with her husband and children. Connect with her at www.Avenue8Advisors.com.

CPSIA information can be obtained
at www.ICGtesting.com
Printed in the USA
LVHW092033230220
647719LV00001BA/1